Rainbow's End

By Bess Forbes Franklin Macdonald Turk

With Susan D. Brandenburg

Acknowledgements

To my treasured children:

Claire, my firstborn, the gifted graphic artist whose ability has contributed to this book. It is heady stuff to be the recipient of her talented love.

Ken, my second-born, who climbed the tree and took the cover photo. With his wife, Hilary, he has graced my life with my two grandchildren, Caden and Tiger.

Lisa, my youngest, "the caretaker" who saved all the pictures years ago by making a scrapbook for me and, because of their preservation, they are ready for use in this book.

My never-ending gratitude:

To Jim Macdonald, my dearest husband and father of my three treasures, shared with me a fascinating life before he died too early.

To Fred Turk, my second husband, picked me up and put me back on my feet a few years after Jim's death.

To Joe Bracewell, who is sharing with me the burden of old age and because of Joe's biography, I was led to meet Susan D. Brandenburg, who is also my Scribe and now dearest friend; and whose talent to "keep me at it" is phenomenal.

To Susanne Schuenke, whose extraordinary artistic talent enriches my life and who is the one who said, "Start writing now!" and I did.

Rainbow's End

I want to see the world from far on high
Over the rainbow and into the sky
I'll spread my wings and simply fly

From icebergs afloat in blue and white
Moonlight a beacon keeping watch by night
Over chalklike Cliffs of Dover
Formed by fossils of ancient life

On to Irish shamrocks and purple Scottish heather
Their modulating hues vary in changing weather
Dunes of the African desert, shifted by sands of Pink
Dry avalanches sliding, taking life to the very brink

As I circle the earth, passing seven seas and more,
Yearning to fly to places I've yet to explore…
A sparkling splash of color I've never seen before,
Transports me to the rainbow at my own front door!

by Bessie Forbes Franklin Macdonald Turk

Table of Contents

Chapter 1: Fall Hill Calls to Me Still 1

Chapter 2: Amoy, China 7

Chapter 3: Barcelona, Spain 11

Chapter 4: Marseilles, France/Bordighera, Italy 14

Chapter 5: Stockholm, Sweden 16

Chapter 6: A Terrifying Trip 19

Chapter 7: Niagra Falls, Canada 21

Chapter 8: St. Anne's 23

Chapter 9: New York City 29

Chapter 10: A Coldwater Flat in the Village 34

Chapter 11: Aix en Provence 39

Chapter 12: London, England 51

Chapter 13: Long Island & Back to England 55

Chapter 14: Paris, France & Genoa, Italy 59

Chapter 15: First Time in Lisbon, Portugal 67

Chapter 16: Return to Paris 76

Chapter 17: New York City Again 81

Chapter 18: Carcavelos, Portugal 84

Chapter 19: A Sad Homecoming 90

Chapter 20: Miracles Make Way for the Future 95

Chapter 21: 210 Brooke Drive 113

Chapter 22: Cameroon 123

Chapter 23: God says Florida? 141

Chapter 24: Cypress Village, My Church Family, My Now! 149

Chapter 25: Bessie's Poetry 154

Chapter 1
Fall Hill Calls to Me Still …

I was born in Saltillo, Mexico on March 11, 1929 with my little heart and soul firmly planted in American soil. My father, Lynn Franklin, was in the U.S. Foreign Service, a diplomat who was regularly sent to the world's trouble spots to calm the winds of war. My mother, Butler Brayne Thornton Robinson Franklin, owned Fall Hill, a 3,000 acre estate in Fredericksburg, Virginia. She had inherited the estate at the age of twelve from her grandfather. Fall Hill, deeded by land grant to the Thornton family of Virginia by King George in the late 1600's, was to become my American anchor during a childhood spent in a whirlpool of foreign adventure, conflict and intrigue.

Construction of the big house at Fall Hill was probably completed around 1740. Beneath its Mansard roof, Fall Hill had four large bedrooms upstairs, a huge central hall and bath, and the same layout downstairs with two parlors on one side and a dining room and smaller bedroom on the other, plus an enormous basement with a fireplace big enough to cook an ox. A wing was later built to house a kitchen and dinette, and this was always dubbed "the new wing" despite the fact that it was at least a century old when I was born.

As with many old historic homes, a ghost is said to roam the halls. An Indian maiden, her name is Katina. She was brought as a teenager to Fall Hill by Governor Spotswood after a skirmish with Indians and remained with the family for the rest of her life taking care of at least three generations of children. My mother saw her many times. She was slender with long black braided hair, patient and loving, a true caretaker, and visited my mother, my grandmother, my father and my uncle. I never saw her. My father saw her walking down the hall. He turned to call thinking it was me, but I was in school. Recently, the new owner/

caretaker of Fall Hill, Maureen Kefauver, was suffering from migraines and she talks of Katina coming in to gently stroke her brow. The migraines went away. There is a book in Fredericksburg on Katina for people who are interested in ghosts. Once, when a couple of "ghost busters" came to the house and offered their services, I politely informed them, "Gentlemen, you may leave. We love our ghost."

On the grounds are two cottages. One was used as the school house and the other, much nearer the house, was the summer kitchen with the ubiquitous huge fireplace that could roast an ox, although I do not recall ever having an ox to roast in either fireplace. The cook lived upstairs in the kitchen cottage and later, mother added an annex to make a bath with running water.

Wherever conflict arose in the world, my father (who was of Quaker heritage) would arrive like the knight in shining armor on a white horse, brandishing the banner of the United States of America. It was fortunate for us that he was a family man as well as a patriot and peacemaker because we were privileged to travel with him to many exotic and wonderful places. Fall Hill was our family's foundation, patiently awaiting our return from wherever in the world we traveled. It is filled with treasured mementos of those travels, even today.

For instance, upon my birth, the mayor of Saltillo (so grateful for the resolution of a conflict over oil rights) presented my father with an iron munitions trunk from the Battle of Santa Anna, made to be carried between mules. Subsequently, we took the trunk to Fall Hill and used it to store all of the flags flown at each consulate where my father served. The trunk signifying my birth still remains at Fall Hill with the American flag stored in it.

Today, the 3,000 acres has dwindled to 22 and Fall Hill has been designated a Landmark of Historic Places (both in the National Register and the Virginia Register). The estate stayed in the family for 250 years with a short hiatus of fifteen years when a family called Hillier bought it. During that time, my great-grandfather, Fred Robinson, was manager of San Simeon, the Hearst estate in California. When he retired, my great-grandfather was asked by Phoebe Hearst to tell her his heart's desire, which was to buy back Fall Hill. He was then given a check in the amount of $25,000 to buy back the estate, which he did.

Chapter 1: Fall Hill Calls to Me Still

Reminders of our many travels became familiar parts of our childhood visits to Fall Hill. For instance, we were in Spain as World War II was looming and my father was reassigned to Sweden, but while still in Spain, my father was asked by a wealthy Spaniard, Mr. Miro, to help secure a visa for him and his family. The Spaniard, who was facing death due to his status, assured my father that he had skills to contribute to America, and my father was thus able to acquire the visas. On leaving Spain, the man came to the consulate and handed my father a small sack of exquisite jewels, including two cameos and two pairs of diamond earrings. He then handed him a larger parcel containing an opera length mink coat with hood. Further, he instructed my father to go to his villa when he was transferred out of Spain and take with him all the furnishings he might want for his home in Virginia, because if the Spaniard had not returned, he would probably either be dead or have escaped with just the clothes on his back.

Father and mother did take the furnishings to Fall Hill and they fit in it splendidly, as one can imagine. The bed set that my sister, Jenny, and I lived with as children visiting Fall Hill was wooden, painted blue with gold raffia inserts, all from Miro's villa. The matching armoire was a work of art – a beautiful European design with one full-length oval mirror in the center and two attached shelved areas on either side, decorated with garlands of carved gilded wood. Inside, the tables, drawers and armoire were lined with curly maple veneer – such a pretty wood.

Another spectacular piece from Miro's estate was the Spanish Boat Bed where our parents slept. It had a curved headboard and footboard sitting on a separate platform to protect from drafts. We could crawl under that bed and hide. Because mother was 5'11" tall, the wood on her side of the footboard was cracked. Father's side was intact, as he was only 5'6." Amazing! I never noticed he was so much shorter. He walked so tall.

About fifteen years after father's death, mother opened the door to Mr. Miro. Standing on the door step at Fall Hill, Miro was a haggard man who requested only that

Rainbow's End

mother agree to give him $2,000, which she did … in payments of $50 per month. It was all she could afford. Mr. Miro disappeared and we never heard from him again.

Father died of a massive heart attack at Fall Hill. He'd had some minor attacks following his early retirement, but the big one was unexpected. He worked too hard trying to fix up that old house – spending hours high on ladders painting. In fact, during his two short years of retirement he was so strenuously attempting to restore Fall Hill that mother would call the doctor but could do nothing to stop him. The doctor advised her to simply stop scolding him. It was his love for Fall Hill that killed him.

There was no pension from my father because the choice that father and mother had made when he retired was to take a lump sum of $10,000 because they needed all of that to continue paying our school fees. After father died, mother did, however, create for herself a social security fund by showing all the receipts that she had over the past twenty years of rentals of cottages and rooms to Quantico Marines. Quantico is only twenty miles from Fredericksburg and she was designated a landlord by that base. With that, she had created her own social security income.

She also went to work as a secretary in Senator Dulles's office after my father died. Working in that atmosphere, she saw the value of lobbying and became a lobbyist herself, championing women's rights of equality. Her particular goal was to get an income for herself from the state department. She did indeed convince congress that widows of foreign service officers should have an income after their husband's died. Up to then, they did not. It is on record that she received a standing ovation from congress. She followed this successful endeavor by marching with Alice Paul, an historic champion of Women's Equal Rights, and attended many functions supporting Alice Paul.

Mother accepted a position to be manager of DACOR Bacon House, a club which is a home-base for foreign service officers who need to "check in" to the State Department from time to time. They can reside there and use the home for necessary

Chapter 1: Fall Hill Calls to Me Still

entertainment. She did all this, commuting from Fall Hill to Washington DC in her grey Volkswagen Bus, into her late seventies.

She founded and organized Historic Fredericksburg. She got the first group together when she noticed that a small toll house near the Rappahannock was being torn down. She walked up to the workers and told them to stop immediately and then went to the powers that be and offered them an exchange. They would let her and her team (which she hadn't gathered yet) have all the bricks from the building and they would reconstruct that little house in a safer place, where it stands today as a tourist attraction. That incident prompted the founding of Historic Fredericksburg, a force that has saved hundreds of historic buildings since. The annual meeting of Historic Fredericksburg is held, to this day, at Fall Hill.

Just as my siblings and I were international citizens (each of us born far from the Virginia hillside that was our family home), I was destined to continue that tradition of raising my children abroad but always returning to my roots in Virginia.

My maternal grandmother, Bessie Forbes Taylor Robinson, whom I called Gran, was at my birth in Saltillo. She lived with our family on a six month basis throughout my childhood, always returning to Fall Hill for the remainder of the year. My brother, Butler, was born in Peking, sister Jenny-Lynn on a ship in the Pacific Ocean, and brother Lynn was born in Marseilles, France. Likewise, my children, Claire, Ken and Lisa were global children who were raised in Europe, but always knew that Fall Hill was home.

Mother adored Fall Hill all of her long life. She lived to be 104 and spent only her last few years in an assisted living facility. Until then, she was firmly entrenched at her beloved estate. When a tree died on the place, a little part of her died with it. She would embrace the dead tree and pray for it.

One day, when she was in her nineties, Mother was sitting on her porch overlooking the town (Fall Hill is on one of the four hills around Fredericksburg). She was watching a storm approach when her tenant from the kitchen cottage, Bob Lowry, came running. A biologist, Bob was alarmed because blacksnakes were leaving the huge oak in front of the main house and coming to the walnut tree in front of his cottage.

Rainbow's End

"Get off the porch and out of the house!" was his frantic warning to mother. She did not move. Within half an hour, a bolt of lightning struck the two-hundred year old oak and a high wind brought it down. It fell toward the town and away from the house. Had it fallen toward the house, it would have destroyed it and anyone in its path. Mother was not at all surprised. She had expected it to happen that way all along and had told us so when we would reprimand her for not having it trimmed to lessen its danger to the house.

My son, Kenneth, once found blacksnake eggs in that oak tree. He bought a small hatchery for his bedroom and hatched them. He kept them in a large fish tank with a heater and piled books on top of it to assure that they would not get out. He raised mice to feed them. One day when he was at school and I was cleaning his room, I removed the books thinking they should go in the bookcase without realizing their purpose, and the snakes escaped. When I told mother, she said, "Good heavens, don't tell the maid! She'll never come back again." The maid was Marie Hawkins, who had been with our family for decades.

A few years later, when we were looking over the need for new insulation in the attic (an extraordinary expense for an attic with the largest beams I've ever seen, holding up a heavy slate roof), we found the rafters hung with hundreds of snake skins. There were no live snakes at this point because they could go in and out from the eaves to the trees, but that's where Ken's snakes had been all these years. It also solved a riddle mother had posed ... why there were no mice at Fall Hill.

When I moved back to Fall Hill with my second husband in the early 1980's, we worked strenuously to do what was needed with a centuries-old house and no family fortune to pay for repairs. Even under the designation of historic landmark, there is small compensation for repairs that require perfect replicas of parts that have disintegrated with time. It is a very costly procedure. Fall Hill is necessarily open to the general public one day a year because of its landmark designation and the present owners are fabulous caretakers. They have brought Fall Hill back to a glory it never even had in the beginning.

Before the American Revolution, Fall Hill was there. It is our country's past and a beautiful heritage to pass on to future generations. It is living history, and so am I.

Chapter 2
Amoy, China

When we departed from Saltillo with father's next assignment being Amoy, China, I was two years old, my brother Butler was five, and my sister, Jenny, was three.

On our visit to Fall Hill prior to fulfilling father's next assignment, I remember my grandfather picking me up, lifting me high in the air, and looking at me with his big burly face. He said, with great glee, "You are so little!" It is the last memory I have of my grandfather, Fred Robinson, Jr., whose father was the man that bought back Fall Hill for $25,000.

My grandparents bid us a fond farewell as we set out to travel by ship across the Pacific Ocean to Amoy, China. On shipboard, we experienced a most frightening storm, teaching me at that early age how violent an opponent the ocean can be. There were no stabilizers in those days and the pitching was literally sickening. I could not leave my bed and remember the water covering the porthole in one second and then looking out at a mountain of water approaching again. At one point I was alone in the stateroom when a big trunk rolled against the door, making my parents frantic when they tried to get in. That moment of terror remained with me always.

In Amoy, we lived at the American Consulate compound, which had a glorious garden and walled-within protection. One side, though, went down to the very edge of the Port of Amoy where we could watch the ships from the safety of the garden.

When I was about four years old, my mother took me with her to the dressmakers on the other side of the harbor. It was a special treat to leave the walls of our American compound in the consulate. Mother and I were nestled into our rickshaw and, while jogging down the street, I saw Chinese children sitting on their doorsteps with their bowls of rice up to their mouth shoveling in the grains with chopsticks the way my nurse forbid me to do. I had been forced to learn to balance all those little pieces with my chopsticks the way any well-raised child would. It was tedious and I longed to put the bowl to my lips and shovel it in.

Rainbow's End

I still remember the smells from the street that I was not used to in my well-kept garden compound, and the delicious cooking odors and fresh fish being grilled on their outdoor hibachis. Other rickshaws passed by, carrying produce and people. There were piles of straw precariously balanced on the rickshaws, little wisps falling off as they jogged their way through the narrow streets. There were toddlers peeing in the street with their pants made so cleverly to split open when they bent over - no diapers for them! It was fascinating to my four-year old eyes. Our coolie called out "Ride, Missies, Ride!" meaning to jog with the rickshaw in rhythm with his step to make his job easier.

We took a ferry across Amoy Harbor to the other side. Our coolie and rickshaw stayed with us. As we crossed the harbor I was thrilled to see a myriad of water transports. One was a sampan with the whole family living on board on a long flat wooden structure with a center cottage. Pets were running around, small children playing, mother in the kitchen, father fishing, laundry hanging on a line and smoke wafting out from the cottage. Then there was the ocean going galleon, a Chinese junk, with the elaborate high back painted in brilliant colors and wonderful Chinese figures, with an eye always painted on the bow. The captain and crew lived in that higher portion of the junk. I recall square sails - probably once white but beige with time, as those ships had plowed the seas. I was later to learn that the Chinese had invented a magnetic compass centuries before we did.

Another floating vessel was the small boat with one triangular sail. It was the work horse of the harbor and did a huge amount of transporting of cargo from ship to shore. Those were the hard-working boats – anything the ships had to take to shore, they transported. This was the time when the west was beginning to gobble up the silk, opium and other treasures of China – a busy, turbulent time in history.

Many birds darted in and out of the activity in the harbor, apparently looking for dropped food between the boats. I later learned that some of the sampan fathers were fishing with skimmer birds (similar to Anhinga's). They would tie a string around the long neck of the bird just tight enough to keep the fish from being swallowed and when the bird caught the fish, the fisherman caught the bird, pulling it in, removing the catch and preparing the fish for dinner.

The small red and white pleasure boats darted easily in and out. Mother didn't explain at the time, but I later learned that those were small vessels of ill-repute, a Chinese version of the red light district.

Chapter 2: Amoy, China

When we arrived at the dressmakers, three or four tiny smiling seamstresses surrounded mother, each of them fetching a box to stand on in order to measure her 5'11" frame. They sat me at a small table and gave me lovely things to play with and ushered our coolie into a back room from where he returned some hours later beaming from ear to ear. He, too, had been well-entertained.

Mother's red silk dress was sensational. She had a choice of many patterns. Recent designs were more expensive than the patterns of years before, so she chose an older pattern. It mattered not to Americans which year's design was chosen – they were all lovely. During the fitting, a seamstress dropped a pair of scissors which fell straight down into mother's toe. I never forgot how mother reacted. Stoically she said, "It's alright – It's alright." She was more worried about their anguish than her own, and with bloody foot bandaged and distressed seamstresses surrounding us with apologies, mother comforted them with a smile and we calmly got back in our rickshaw for the ride home.

That dress lasted for at least forty years. I remember her wearing it in Canada when she was asked to appear at many civic events to lecture on her experiences in China. For a brief time in Canada, she hosted her own radio show, telling the stories of China each week. She was a natural orator and could have been a professional speaker had we not constantly been on the move. Whenever she lectured on China, she wore her red silk dress. It was elegant Chinese style, with the high mandarin color and covered frog buttons crossing over from one shoulder to the other and down one side, making a sheath to the floor. With that dress, she always wore scrimshawed ivory and cinnabar beads that she had knotted for herself in China. I wear those beads still.

Many years later, my sister, Jenny, painted a portrait of Mother in that dress, wearing those beads and holding a magnifying glass. Today, I also hold a magnifying glass due to the macular degeneration that both of us developed in our later years. The magnifying glass is just one symbol of the many parallels between my mother's life and mine.

A serious incident that my mother had to deal with while in Amoy happened with her number one boy – the servant that reported directly to her and literally ran the household at her direction. Mother had gone to the kitchen only to discover her number one boy sitting at a table with about six Japanese men, sharing my father's top-secret papers. The servant was subsequently punished as a spy and mother was faced with the huge task of reorganizing her household and had to find another number one house boy.

Rainbow's End

As the American Consul to China, father had inside information on the impending attack of Japan. I remember playing in the walled-in garden of the consulate and seeing the armada of Japanese warships anchored in Amoy Harbor. That summer, we traveled to a home in the hills to "get away from the heat," but there came a night when my Amah hustled my siblings and me out of bed with urgent whispers, "Come on … be quick … don't dress … just get in the rickshaw … make no noise!" As our family was being pulled down the hill, I looked back to see a stream of lanterns being carried by bandits on foot preparing to attack our villa, which they thought was unoccupied. It was a terrifying sight that I internalized as a young child, later discovering that it was the basis for my lifelong panic at the sight of any unified group approaching me.

When I was five years old, father was assigned to Barcelona, Spain, where a civil war was churning. As was our habit, we returned to Fall Hill for a brief respite before traveling on to Spain.

Chapter 3
Barcelona, Spain

My first memory of Barcelona was the beautiful garden that surrounded our large home. There were terraces on each floor shaded a huge fig tree. My siblings and I were quickly scrambling up it and happily eating the ripe fruit. Give me a ripe purple plum from a tree today and it will take me right back to Barcelona.

Soon, I met our cook, Lola, and the maid and chauffer. All three of them became very dear to me. The arrival of our tutor from England marked the beginning of our home schooling.

I spent as much time as I could in the kitchen with Lola. I loved to cook with her. She always made me a 4 o'clock snack of fresh bed with a big piece of chocolate melting in the warmth of

the bread. It is still one of my favorite snacks. Lola and I would sing together – beautiful Spanish songs – while mother and grandmother took Flamenco dancing lessons upstairs. The songs that we sang and the Flamenco music of Barcelona sometimes flavor the songs I write today. I now wear the shawl my grandmother bought for her Flamenco dancing lessons and Mother kept her high Spanish combs for many years.

On one of the terraces, we had an eight foot tall, three foot wide cage filled with dozens of yellow canaries. They were my grandmother's hobby. At mating time, she would boil an egg, mash the yoke, add special seed and put the mixture into the food dish. She said it helped strengthen the egg shells. We children would search the Barcelona beach for fresh cuttlebones (the center backbone of an octopus) which washed up with the tide. The canaries loved to nibble the cuttlebones, which seemed to help with digestion and sharpening their beaks. Sometimes the canaries would escape as they were being fed, and grandmother would call out to us, "Find the canaries! Find the canaries!" We loved it! A chance to scramble up every tree we could climb, with no restrictions or calls out to be careful. Just "Find the canaries!" We always did. After all, they didn't really want to leave.

Jenny almost drowned one day when we went to the public swimming pool. As I was being given swimming lessons, the life guard called out for help and dived into the water, pulling up my sister, Jenny. He had seen her lying on the bottom of the pool. She was quickly rescued and thoroughly recovered, but it did not help me want to learn to swim.

One day, Jenny developed a horrible boil on the back of her neck. The doctor performed surgery on it right there in the house with no anesthetic. I remember the horror of her screaming at the top of her lungs and all the mess of the surgery. Medicine has changed a great deal since then, thank God.

In 1937, the Nationalists, under the leadership of Francisco Franco began to establish their dominance and the Spanish Civil War began. Hemingway based his book, For Whom the Bells Toll, on this war, and Picasso's famous Guernica painting was a result of this time in history. Communism and anarchy reigned and our lives drastically changed. It became unsafe even within our home, as sniper planes were shooting into the house and we often had to crawl under windows to go from room to room. I never remember feeling in danger. Mother made crawling beneath the windows just a game. Dad made arrangements for us and all other Americans to evacuate to Marseilles, France. Mother remained amazingly calm throughout this ordeal, despite the fact that she was nine months pregnant with my brother, Lynn. My grandmother was with us, too, as she had joined us from Fall Hill to be there for the birth.

We were piled into our family car – chauffeur, cook and mother in the front seat, grandmother, dad and us three children in the back. The chauffeur had draped an American flag down onto the top of the car tying it securely and hoping that it would protect us from the anger in the streets. As we drove down Las Ramblas toward the Port, we passed bonfires burning looted church artifacts. Priests were running and crying and trying to retrieve their precious treasures, and in one moment, a huge Bible, marvelously illustrated, all hand-written, landed in mother's lap, thrown into the open window by a priest who yelled in English, "Save this! Save this!" The singed edges were still smoking, the burning smell ominous. Our chauffeur was terrified, his hands trembling on the wheel. "No senora, you'll be killed! Throw it back." I remember hearing the word Muerta … but mother did not throw it back, and we kept it for years.

Chapter 4: Marseilles, France/Bordighera, Italy

On arriving at the port, we were ushered up a steep gangplank. I remember the openings between the slats were very wide and the black water below terrified me. I felt I had little to hold on to and my foot could easily slip between. As we turned around to wave goodbye, I realized my father, the cook and the chauffeur were not to be coming with us. It's difficult to describe my lost feelings at that moment. I felt abandoned. My grandmother's arms came around my shoulders and held me tight. She was always my strength, and I believed I was her special darling.

The cook, Lola, and I tried to stretch our hands to touch each other because I truly loved her like a mother. We thought we were seeing one another for the last time, but some twenty-five years later, I was told that a foreign service officer who was with my father had kept Lola in his employ, bringing her to Washington D.C. on retirement and building her a little house in his backyard. I visited her shortly before her death and our reunion closed the space in time. I felt like a little girl and she felt like the same Lola. We embraced and cried. It was so wonderful to find her. I'd lost so many people while moving around the world that reconnecting with one of them was an exquisite experience.

Rainbow's End

Chapter 4
Marseilles, France/Bordighera, Italy

When we arrived in Marseilles, mother booked rooms for us in a pension (small inn) on the sea around the Bay of Marseilles overlooking the Chateau D'If. This was ominous to me, even as a young child, as I was told the Chateau was a prison. Located on the island of If, the smallest island in the Frioul Archipelago and situated one mile from shore in the Mediterranean Sea, the Chateau is famous for being inescapable. It is one of the settings of Alexander Dumas' adventure novel, The Count of Monte Cristo.

The pension was prepared for mother with great excitement, as the staff knew that she was imminently giving birth. We were given comfortable rooms and were welcomed warmly into the dining room. They loved children and made a fuss over us. Often, when I traveled later with my own children, I found that certain people and places made children very happy and certain ones did not. This was one where we children were pampered and accepted as though we were members of their family. I remember a dessert – a mound of creamy white sprinkled with raw sugar. I dipped in my spoon and just went MMMMMMMM. It was bare, fresh goat cheese, snowy and creamy and I loved it so that they gave it to me every night as my special treat. Their kindness went a long way toward salving the wounds of separation, although missing my father and Lola never completely went away.

Mother gave birth four days after arriving in Marseilles, having been transferred to a clinic in town. Grandmother took us to see our new baby brother and we were aghast that he was in my mother's arms, wrapped from neck to toe with what looked like bandages. We were terrified that there was something wrong with him, but this was the normal procedure for newborns in France, and I believe it still is. The baby was calm, suckled well, and my mother's face beamed with victorious delight. She immediately announced that his name was Lynn, after our father. About ten days later, mother and baby came back to the pension and Lynn became a part of our daily routine which was playing and cooing with him, running outdoors, having naps and eating lovely food, attended by the doting staff.

During this time, mother was researching schools for her three older children, as it became apparent that Dad was going to be in Spain for quite a long time. We had no idea if it would be months or years. Wars are like that.

Chapter 5: Stockholm, Sweden

Mother found an international school in Bordighera, Italy on the coast not far from Genoa. She, grandmother and Lynn took up residence in Bordighera, and we children went to the school in the hills above the town. We students were all together with no separation of grades that I can remember. It seems that somehow each of us was taught to our level. We were boarded at the school with dozens of other equally displaced students from all over Europe, including Jewish children from Germany and Austria.

While in that boarding school I was allowed to have a little pet mouse. He came to me one day to nibble some crumbs that had fallen from my bed after sneaking biscuits from the dining room table. He was white, he needed me and I loved him immediately. I was going to be sure to take care of him, so each day I put a treat in front of his hole. It didn't take long for him to start coming more often and our dorm mistress began to notice droppings. I confessed what was happening, and begged her to let me keep him. I named him Squeaky and pretty soon my nickname from my dorm friends was Squeaky. Squeaky would follow me out to the playground which was actually a marvelous ancient walled in courtyard, and he would walk along the high wall.

Mention of the wall leads to another memory that is not so pleasant. As we students were taking a walk in the lovely hills that climbed up from the Mediterranean Sea, our path was edged by a three foot wall. The wall was probably about my height and I was sorely tempted to climb it, as I loved to climb. Up I went, and down I fell! The other side of the wall, I was to discover, was more like eight feet to the field below and I cut my chin seriously as I hit it on a rock and banged my back memorably. Of course, I was soon rescued and became the center of attention for quite a few days. I still have that scar under my chin and odd back problems have often reminded me of that fall.

On my 9th birthday, while still at school in Bordighera, I was given a children's traveling trunk, blue and white. When placed on end it was about as tall as I was and it opened to become a closet – with a place to hang clothing on one side and drawers on the other. I did not expect to use it so soon, but within the year, our family was moved to Sweden and my little trunk became my wardrobe.

Chapter 5
Stockholm, Sweden

As Spain's civil war came to an end, Dad was transferred to Stockholm, Sweden as the American Consul General. He came to Bordighera to get us and saw his newborn son for the first time. Lynn was a full year old by then.

It was when they came to get us at the International School in Bordighera that headmaster Peter Ray begged my parents to help him get his Jewish students to safety and gratefully accepted their offer to transfer his entire school to Fall Hill for the duration of the war.

Saying goodbye to my little mouse Squeaky was more difficult than I can explain. It was, once more, a painful separation that seemed more than I was able to bear. By age nine, I had obviously developed separation anxiety that was quite deep. In fact, as I write this memoir, more than seven decades later, I realize that never in my lifetime of leaving places have I officially attended or been given a "going away party." Ah well, Squeaky probably escaped into the wild and had a lovely life.

In Stockholm, there was no formal housing for state department employees. My parents chose a beautiful villa out in the countryside bordering the North Sea. The remote location of our home was chosen because my father was experiencing serious emotional trauma due to the stress of the Spanish civil war. He hadn't lost one American – which was a huge feat and a huge task that now laid him low. The stress of civil war and separation from family had taken its toll. Nowadays, we'd call it post-traumatic syndrome. The doctor in Sweden suggested to my mother that she choose a home in the country, hire as much staff as she could, whether she could afford it or not, and take my father for long walks every day. That prescription cured him.

Our staff included a new English tutor, a nurse for Lynn, a maid and a cook, and a chauffeur to get Dad to the office. That's a chunk of change … but far better than anti-depressants. No side affects. Soon, Dad returned to his loving, happy, whistling self. I had never realized until then how much a part of my life his perpetual whistling was and how much I had missed the sound of it when he was not there.

We children and the tutor went skiing constantly because the trails were marked and went by the house. We could have skied all the way to Norway if we wanted to go. I remember the trail by our house was yellow, indicating the degree of difficulty – there

Chapter 5: Stockholm, Sweden

were blue trails and red trails, as I recall. We could even see the high ski jump that was being prepared for the memorable 1936 Olympics, when the world met Hitler.

Before we left for a day of skiing our tutor always insisted that we drink a glass of milk with a raw egg plopped into the bottom because it would give us the stamina we would need. I found that drink impossible to swallow, and he would take the other two children and go out, saying, "When you've drunk it, join us, and if you don't drink it, you don't come." My brother Butler would scoot around from the maid's entrance, swallow it for me, and then we'd take off. My sister, Jenny, was in on the cover-up. We were a close band of three.

One day we nearly panicked because our little toddler, Lynn, had taken off, pushing my doll's stroller onto the snowy trail and disappearing. He was found after much searching, of course, but it was a harbinger of his future proclivity to run away, which he did throughout his short life. Lynn added a magical element of fun to our lives, always, and one of his lasting influences was his inability as a toddler just learning to talk to pronounce the word Mother. Instead, he mouthed "Muzzie," and that adorable nickname stuck with our mother for the rest of her life. We all began to call her "Muzzie." One Christmas when Lynn was in his twenties, he came to Fall Hill to celebrate and brought mother a heavy red flannel jogging suit embroidered with the word "Muzzie" on the rear in fat wool stitches. She wore it for years.

When the North Sea froze up, the government announced the thickness of the ice every morning on the radio. We bought a Swedish sled with runners about eight feet long and a wooden seat. It was similar to an Alaskan dog sled and we could put grandmother on the sled, holding little Lynn on her lap, and push her around the North Sea "rink." This was a clearing made by neighbors far and near to create a large, smooth rink on the ice. Many parties were held down there with hot drinks (toddies for adults and chocolate for children). Sledding and ice-skating were as common there as barbecuing in the back yard is in America.

By the next year, Dad had completely recovered from his stress and we moved to an apartment in the City of Stockholm to be near the consulate. Our staff was dramatically reduced to a maid and tutor. Living in the city was much different.

Jenny and I were walking home one day after taking an extracurricular class in the Swedish language, and a gang of teenage girls started following us. They were teasing us with anti-American remarks and, at one point, they pushed a ruler between my sister's legs to make her trip. When she got up, we took each other's hands and dashed up the street towards an open door in an apartment building. On entering, we slammed into a chauffeur coming to get his boss's car. His boss had just arrived in the lobby and when we told them what was happening, he put us in his car, telling the chauffeur to chase those girls and give them a good scare. He then asked where we lived and was delighted to hear we were American, and also the Consul General's daughters. At home, he met my father and mother, who invited him for dinner. That gentleman who came to our rescue became a good friend to our family for the remainder of our stay in Sweden.

We were in Sweden for nearly four years and it must have been peaceful because all I remember are lovely ski trips, constant ice skating, and delightful lessons with our tutor. I loved being homeschooled. Mother used the Calvert curriculum and it was effective - especially the text books. I remember our history book had an illustration by Antoine de Saint Exupery of a little boy sitting on the edge of a planet looking at the earth through binoculars. My favorite of his books was The Little Prince, which contained the quote: "Here is my secret. It is very simple. It is only with the heart that one can see rightly. What is essential is invisible to the eye."

The Calvert books were easy to read and so informative. It was never a burden to do homework. I would look forward to it. There was so much to learn. I even loved the quarterly events of supplies arriving from the Calvert School with fresh pads of paper (they smelled so good), packs of number 2 pencils with erasers and, of course, those wonderful text books. But life was to be learned beyond the textbooks, too, and our next move would prove to give us some sad and memorable lessons along the way.

Chapter 6
A Terrifying Trip

Dad's next post was Niagra Falls, Canada, which meant a train ride through Europe to the Port of Genoa, Italy, and a ship to New York, and another visit to Fall Hill before we arrived at our next assignment.

It was 1940, and our trip through Europe was, regrettably, quite eventful. Once we crossed the North Sea by boat, we all took our places in the Wagon Lits (sleeper car on the train). Our first stop was Berlin, Germany. Mother wanted to visit her dearest friend, Nanna, who had been with her husband in the German Embassy in Stockholm. They had been recalled to Germany to serve Hitler, their son to join the Nazi Air Force. Nanna had gone reluctantly.

Upon arriving in Berlin, Mother called Nanna to come to the hotel and, if she could, to bring her darling little Pekinese that we children adored. As Mother and Nanna had tea in one room, we played with the Pekinese in the other. We ran under the beds and around the tables, playing joyfully with the little dog, and in the process of playing, found little black buttons attached to many of the chair legs and lamps. Later, after Nanna left, we pointed them out to Mother and discovered that they were hidden microphones, but it was too late. Nanna had wept and told Mother everything about what had happened when they returned to Germany. Her son and husband had become estranged because of their different ideology and she was virtually ignored. We never heard from her again.

The next day we boarded the train again to go to Genoa. This time, during the night, grandmother and I were harassed. The conductor knocked on our door five times at least to demand our passports. Dad had told us never to let go of them, so we didn't. A fellow passenger confided to us later that the conductor suspected grandmother of being a Jew because she knitted in the European fashion with her left hand rather than the American way of pulling the wool over the needle with the right hand. Imagine the tenuous position of every civilian if a small detail like that could put you into Auschwitz.

Rainbow's End

Every station along the way was dense with passengers clamoring to board the train. There was never enough room for everyone. I remember all those desperate faces peering into the train as we closed the doors and pulled away from the station.

After what seemed like an endless train ride, we boarded a Cunard liner and sailed for America. Within nine days, we arrived in New York. At the bottom of the gangplank, my mother knelt down on that dirty concrete and kissed America.

Chapter 7
Niagra Falls, Canada

We went for a short visit to Fall Hill before driving to Niagra Falls, Canada in our new long grey Buick. We were delighted with the space we had in comparison to our European cars.

Our first home was a small house in the town without much garden, but Dad soon found a much better home. In fact, it was the "Gate Cottage" (some cottage … it had five bedrooms) for the Oakes estate next door. The estate has since become a well-known hotel, as it directly overlooks both the American and the Canadian falls, but at the time we lived there, the Oakes family was still in residence. Rumor had it that the senior Mr. Oakes had been murdered when his bed suspiciously caught on fire. The son-in-law was suspected of setting the fire but it was never proven. He left for South America after the death of Mr. Oakes, and the family inherited the estate.

Our perpetual view was that magnificent wonder of the world called Niagra Falls. Lit at night, the changing colors kept Jenny and me absolutely mesmerized, as our second-floor bedroom faced that view.

The gate cottage had a barn and Dad made use of it by buying us a donkey and a darling small raffia cart that seated five. We could even take it across the Rainbow Bridge over the Niagra River into the park nearby. No special license was required, which was ridiculous – Jenny was only fourteen and I was thirteen. Once in a while, we'd take some boyfriends with us across the Rainbow Bridge. The round trip was about two hours with no pit stops along the way. For a teenage girl, that was sometimes a challenge.

Our tutor went back to England when we left Sweden, so Jenny, Lynn and I were enrolled in the convent in Niagra Falls, called the Loretto Academy. The nuns would tuck their skirts up into their belts and play sports with us, running better than any of us.

One memorable nun teacher had taught at a Loretto Academy in China and one morning she was so frustrated with our lack of attention that she banged her book on the desk in an uncharacteristic display of temper and said, " taught for thirteen years to children who would walk, barefoot, to come to school, and I can't even get your attention!" She certainly got my attention and I discovered she was an excellent history teacher.

Rainbow's End

Lynn was entered into the pre-school and, at one point, was asked by a student if he was Catholic. He didn't know. So the student said, "If you're not Catholic, you'll go to Limbo." Lynn's young mind processed that to mean hell and he ran away. He found his way home by skirting the shores of the falls until he came to the hill on which our house was built. He climbed towards the house, wet and cold, after falling into a pond below. When he finally got home, he asked my distressed mother where limbo was and if he was going there. It had to have been a terrifying trek over three miles of dangerous terrain, but he somehow made it home. It seems that Lynn was courting death from the day he was born.

While in Canada, we had trouble with our dog, Tupper, a black and white water spaniel who had been given to our father by the departing consul. That dog loved water and would regularly run away and jump into the turbulent waters of the shore below where the Maid of the Mist Ferries were docked. The ferries took tourists into white water currents of the falls, handing each tourist a heavy parka to wear. Tupper would regularly be fished out by the security guards at the Maid of the Mist docks and brought home. They all soon recognized Tupper. Even crossing bridges on our frequent trips to Fall Hill with Tupper would cause him to whine and try to leap out of the car into the water. He finally died from overexerting himself as he swam in the Rappahannock which borders Fall Hill on the east.

Canada was wonderful for us during the war. It was peaceful for our family, and Dad was inundated by European refugees trying to enter the United States through Canada. One of those refugees was Henri Soulee, a French Chef who subsequently became very successful in New York and Long Island and treated our family to meals when we visited his restaurant, Le Pavillon.

During our stay in Canada, Mother began a regular radio program telling stories of China, which was then of great interest to the west. At the time, it was an exotic unknown and its secrecy was being cracked by Japan's attack and the emergence of communism. Americans were eager to know about its treasures and its culture. Mother also began her lecture circuit on China, always wearing that beautiful red dress when she lectured. That came to an end, however, when Dad was transferred to Curacao, located in the West Indies off the Coast of Venezuela and next to Aruba. It was the only Dutch property that was still free from the German conquest of Holland.

Chapter 8
St. Anne's

At age fourteen, I made the decision that I wanted to stay on American soil instead of traveling with my family to my father's next post in the West Indies. I asked him to please allow me to stay in Virginia, and my parents found St. Anne's Boarding School in Charlottesville (right next to the University of Virginia).

It was at St. Anne's that I picked up more information about the facts of life than I had ever been taught by my mother. One night, following one of our tea dances, which were held regularly to instruct us in the social graces, I was called into the office of the head mistress privately while all of the other girls were called into an assistant's office. Apparently, an incident had occurred during the dance with one of the students and her boyfriend. Being singled out terrified me as I felt I must be the culprit, but the head mistress, Miss Cochran, with great wisdom, seemed to know that I was not ready for the very frank discussion they were having with the other girls. She was astute, and with tact and careful wording, she explained to me the possibilities of arousing a dance partner and I left better informed but not afraid. I really suspect that my regular dance partner and date, Les Fuller (who I'd met at a previous tea dance) was as naïve as I was. We danced primly and never had a problem, concentrating on steps rather than sex.

I had hopes at that time of becoming a modern dancer and had been inspired by a teacher St. Anne's employed who was Martha Graham's most promising performer. She had given up her career to marry a professor at the University of Virginia and therefore was available as a teacher for us at St. Anne's. For me, it was the excitement of the dance, not the date. In fact, during Christmas vacation one year when we had a big dance party at Fall Hill, my date, who was an aspiring poet from Fredericksburg and madly in love with me, took me out on the front porch and told me, "Bessie. I think you're terribly naïve." I didn't want sex. I simply wanted to dance.

Rainbow's End

While my parents were stationed in Curacao, the arrangement was that Mother and Lynn would come up for Christmas because both my brother and sister were at college in America. Butler was at VMI and Jenny was at American University, both within driving distance of Fredericksburg. This arrangement made it possible for only one fare had to be paid to America and we children to be together at Fall Hill for Christmas. That became a pattern.

One notable year, the Governor of Curacao's family joined us at Fall Hill for Christmas as their oldest son, Franz, was also at VMI with Butler and their daughter, Annamieka, was at American University with my sister. Mother had already arranged a kitchen in the upstairs which she sometimes rented as an apartment when she was away, so she let Governor Kasteel's family have the upstairs and we had the downstairs, happily combining mealtimes and family celebrations. Temporary romances abounded that Christmas. Butler fell in love with Annamieka and Franz fell in love with me. The families were so compatible, even our younger brothers were friends.

Mrs. Kasteel adored my mother, as she had been instrumental in our government finding her and the children in Holland, where they had been in hiding since the Nazis had invaded in 1940. The Governor had told my father about the plight of his family. In the first year of Dad's service in Curacao, he was invited to the White House as is customary with a new position abroad for a Consul General, and Dad and Mother were at the table with President and Mrs. Roosevelt. Mother was telling Mrs. Roosevelt about the fact that Mrs. Kasteel and the children were trapped in Holland. Mrs. Roosevelt immediately beckoned her husband by waving her hand and saying, "Oh, Franklin dear, listen to this story that Mrs. Franklin has to tell." Mother told our president about the trapped family and he said, "We'll see about that immediately." Within three months, the FBI found them by spotting the oldest son riding into Amsterdam on a bike and followed him back to the cellar of a farmhouse and verified this was the family they were looking for. Successful arrangements were made for them all to get to Curacao. On their joyous arrival of this family in Curacao, the interesting similarity of ages of the children prompted us to become best friends. Jenny, Butler and I actually spent most of our free time at the Governor's palace when we were in Curacao.

I was at St. Anne's for three years and I loved our teachers, especially the history teacher. She cared enough to help me when I failed a final exam just before graduating. In her wisdom, she realized that I did not know how to study. I had the facts and did not know how to put them down. We had a long evening session where she showed me how to organize my information and helped me remember it. I spent most of the night studying that textbook and she gave me another exam in the morning. I passed it with an A. I will always be so grateful to her for teaching me how to organize and look up facts and study correctly. I guess homeschooling had never emphasized self-study because someone was always hovering over our shoulders, with one on one instruction.

As I recall, my grades were mediocre and my teachers were always saying, "Bess, you could do better," but after that long night prior to graduation, I realized that I had never learned how to study until that moment.

During those summers while I was at St. Anne's, my siblings and I sailed on a Dutch tanker to Curacao, and we spent so much time basking in the sun that we would come back nearly black. At the beginning of the new school term, mother would put a note in my passport indicating that I was white, because on the train to Virginia, the colored people were put in a special car, or on the bus in the back. I was definitely that dark, because one day in the train station in New York, I sat down next to a black girl reading Ebony Magazine and she turned around to chat about the magazine, thinking I was also black.

My greatest delight was being in the St. Anne's Glee Club and when I was elected president, it pulled my self-esteem to a high level because when meetings were held with the presidents of groups like Latin, History, School Newspaper, French Club, etc., I was now "one of the chosen." was also chosen to help the instructor of the younger children in dance and we would put on a splendid Maypole dance in the spring.

One of the little children, an extravert and a non-conformist, said to me just before the Maypole dance, where each of the dancers held a ribbon attached to the pole, "Miss Bessie, what would happen if I dropped the ribbon?" I answered, "Just keep on dancing without it so the others don't get mixed up." She did just as she had planned and only I knew that she had been planning it all along. For the Maypole dance, we wore lovely flowing white dresses and ribbons in our hair.

A mischievous friend in the dorm once decided to annoy us all by eating masses of fresh garlic which absolutely stank up the dorm room – to her pleasure and our great annoyance. We couldn't think of anything to retaliate because she was so imaginative, she'd outdo us and we knew it.

Rainbow's End

In the evenings, I'd often find myself painfully homesick and sorry that I'd chosen to go to boarding school, but by morning, with the bright faces of my friends around, I would recover. There was one very embarrassing day as we went to regular morning Chapel that I went in the chapel with a bag of laundry under my arm as I had forgotten to drop it off. As I walked down the aisle to my pew, the bag broke and I dropped the dirty laundry onto the red carpet. That incident came to mind strongly decades later when in a choir procession at my church in Jacksonville Beach, Florida. I was wearing a colostomy bag for a short period after a problem with a surgical procedure and had not attached the Velcro straps correctly. They pulled loose as I walked down the aisle in my choir robe and I scooped up the bag as quickly as possible and exited the church. Thank God the bag was sealed tightly. They told me later that our choir director mouthed to them, "Where's Bess? She was right behind me." They could only indicate that I had left suddenly.

My father once chaperoned me to a dance at VMI while I was a student at St. Anne's. He came to school to pick me up and drive me to Lexington, staying in the town during the dance weekend. He had insisted that he, not my date, would drive me to the dance and pick me up. I am so glad he did because I learned by eavesdropping that my date had planned to drive me out to a small cottage in the country and, by having my father hovering around, I was saved from possible date rape.

There was a big formal graduation ceremony with all of us wearing beautiful white dresses. I was so relieved and happy. A lot of girls were crying, but I was ready to get on with life. The next step for me was to join my sister and brother on a tanker in New York City to sail to Curacao for the summer.

My father had made friends with the Captain of a Dutch tanker and I'm sure had made a good financial deal to transport his children back and forth. We were the only passengers. In the evenings, we would dance on the deck, listening to the swish of gasoline under our feet while the stars shone and the flying fish flew. The crew was our orchestra and they played the marvelous tin drums from the islands. My brother, Butler, and I practiced many complicated steps to show off at the dances in Curacao.

Our summer consisted mostly of swimming and dancing. My sister and I were very popular as the island had an Air Force base, a Marine base, and an Army base. The island was filled with American GI's mainly because there was an enormous oil refinery there that needed to be protected. Dad would chaperone us to every party and, thank goodness for that, because I needed him. I was ripe for adventure and still quite naïve. It was just a wonder in my heart that the young men hovered around us like hummingbirds to the syrup.

At one officer's party, a lieutenant asked me to take his arm and then led me to the bar, but almost instantly there was my father tapping the lieutenant on the shoulder and saying, "My daughter does not come to the bar. Would you please take her to the table?" And, in that gentle way, my father taught me how to behave.

The swimming in Curacao was confined to a beautiful country club where a heavy net enclosed the safe swimming area because barracuda and shark were frequent visitors. We never swam anywhere else. It was just too dangerous. What fascinated me was that the trees around the island all grew bent over like old men because of the constant Mistral trade winds. I had heard about the famous orange liquor called Quantro had begun from their marvelous trees, but there were none there when I was there and I was told that the early crop had been demolished by goats on the island that had devastated the vegetation.

One other thing our father told us when we arrived in Curacao was "never run, girls, it's just too hot." The trade winds blew all year except for during the month of September and made life in the shade very comfortable. In spite of it, my sister and I sunbathed like crazy – always turning nearly black. That was well before we were aware of the dangers of sun exposure.

That summer after graduation, my father needed extra help in the consulate and asked my sister and me to fill in. It was my first taste of a real job and I hated the regular hours, the restrictions on my time and the demands of the bosses. I hoped I'd never have to do that again. I'd already decided to go into dancing, so that desk job confirmed for me that my goals were in the right direction.

Jenny set up a studio upstairs in our home in Curacao where she could paint en plain air and look out at the ocean. We had a pet monkey that lived in the yard and three times in a row, Jenny found her painting smudged. Of course, she blamed Lynn, who insisted he did not do it. It was weeks before we caught the monkey in action, sitting on the easel with a paint brush copying Jenny. Our house was on the ocean, catching the breezes and the servant's houses were on either side of the garden with a wall and a gate to the ocean. They had a bathroom, but never used the tub, and bathed in the sea.

Rainbow's End

The treasure, though, that mother found in the unused tub in the servant's quarters is now in evidence at Fall Hill. In that bathtub, forgotten for years, were hundreds of pieces of Waterford Crystal that the previous owner had apparently gotten tired of keeping clean due to the salt water surroundings. When Mother and Dad put them all together, they recreated three magnificent chandeliers. The landlord was delighted with them and of course we hung them in the home there, but he generously let Mother and Dad keep them and take them to Fall Hill. Those chandeliers are at Fall Hill today and are all still lit by candlelight.

When I graduated, Dad retired and he and mother came to Fall Hill to live. While in Curacao he had had a warning heart attack and decided to retire early. I entered Mary Washington College in Fredericksburg, which was known for dance.

There, I discovered that my body was really not suited for dancing. My knees were not strong enough and my stamina wasn't strong enough, either. I had been singing for fun all my life, from the minute I woke up until I went to bed at night, so I decided to take singing lessons. My family encouraged me in that direction. Because of it, though, I was soon anxious to go to New York where I could concentrate only on singing. So, at age eighteen, I fled Mary Washington College to study music in New York City.

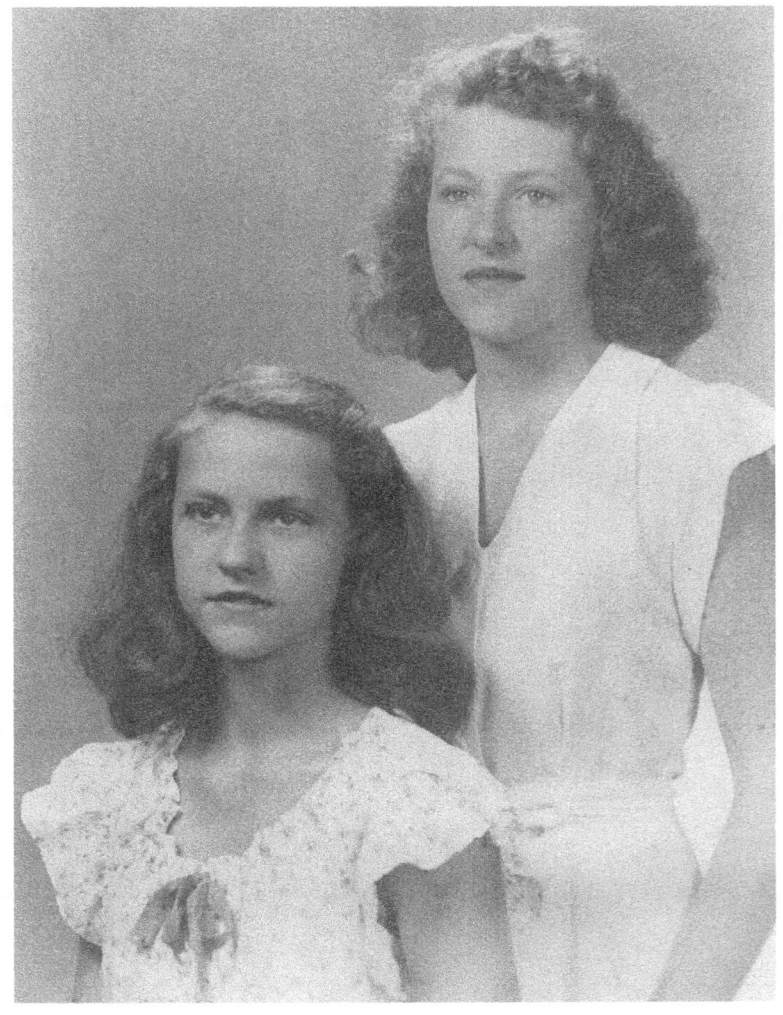

Chapter 9
New York City

Mother's closest friend, Nell Drew, lived in New York City with her husband, Walter. They were a loving, wealthy, philanthropic couple who encouraged Jenny and me to come live with them and they would sponsor us in our pursuit of the arts. My sister went to the Art Students League for classes in painting and I went to a singing teacher who had taught renowned Italian opera singer Galli Curci. The teacher was, by then, very old and really didn't teach me much at all, as it turned out he was living on the fame of his one main student. After a few lessons, I asked Nell if she would find me another teacher, which she did. My next teacher, however, was one that she had sponsored to come to New York with his wife from Russia. Although he spoke perfect English, he merely taught me some new songs and no basics about singing. Aunt Nell had been hopeful about his talents because she had hired him to teach her also, as she had always wanted to be a singer.

Nell and Walter's nine room apartment on 72nd Street and Broadway, with the elevator opening directly into their front hall, was right across the street from the Ansonia Hotel, which is still a magnet for singers. In Aunt Nell's apartment were gathered not only my sister and me, but her niece, Patsy, and Patsy's chaperone, Jeanie. Patsy, who was from Richmond, had a penchant for picking up strange men and needed more attention than her parents could give her. In order to keep her niece in line, Nell had hired Jeanie, an aspiring singer, to be Patsy's companion. Jeanie took singing lessons while Patsy attended drama school.

Mother and Aunt Nell became devoted friends when they were in their early twenties and shared a New York apartment together when Aunt Nell was still seriously pursuing a singing career. Mother had taken a job at the desk of the YMCA, organizing the rental of their rooms. During their stay in New York, Nell had a friend, Julia, back in Richmond, Virginia, who was studying to be a concert pianist. Julia was Nell's age and when Nell heard she'd had a nervous breakdown before her official piano premiere, she immediately went to Richmond to visit her. She found Julia in an asylum, animal-like and angry. Nell begged Julia's parents to let her take her troubled friend back with her to New York so that she could attempt to rehabilitate her.

It was a tremendously brave and frightening offer that the parents gratefully accepted. Julia went to New York to live with Nell and my mother. The two of them took in this wild Julia, and they did manage to tame her to a point of being able to live somewhat "normally." Julia remained with Nell for the rest of her life. She died at about forty-eight. So, Julia was there when we came to New York to live with Aunt Nell in that very full and busy apartment. One of our duties was to make sure that Julia did not escape down the elevator, which she attempted to do every time someone arrived. Julia was given a singing lesson every day by the same Russian teacher who was teaching me. While she was singing, she would seem so normal and say such wise things, but when she wasn't singing, she acted rather crazy and incoherent. She was never violent, though, and we all knew that was as a result of the love Mother and Nell had trained her to accept.

Because of Julia, Aunt Nell insisted on a concert performance every Friday of all the people she sponsored, with as many guests as we wanted to invite. We all had to perform something – even the artists had to display or talk about their art.

Uncle Walter Drew was also a great mentor who made it his business to take me under his wing and share his love of art with me. We would walk to the Metropolitan Museum of Art across Central Park and he would point out to me the styles of different artists. One of his tests was to stop at the doorway of an exhibit and see if I could just look around from a distance and point out who the artists were. He gave me a tremendous gift of knowledge that I still enjoy. He also knew literature and discussed great books with me, and he was a lay student of astronomy and loved to read our horoscopes daily.

Also, Uncle Walter shared with me the simple facts of high finance. He was a multi-millionaire, and once remarked, "Oh, a million doesn't go very far these days." One morning, his broker called at 6 a.m. and Jeannie, Peggy's caretaker, answered the phone and told the broker that Uncle Walter was not to be disturbed, but she would give him the message to call his broker. At about ten a.m. Uncle Walter woke up as was his habit (he and Aunt Nell generally stayed up all night and slept late). When Jeannie gave him the message about the 6 a.m. call from his broker, I saw him furious for the first and only time. He loudly informed all of us that any message for him was urgent. He declared, "Do you know, young ladies, that you cost me almost a million dollars?" He had missed a buy/sell opportunity.

Aunt Nell took care of so many people. She'd be on the phone all night long with all the people she cared about. She was a Christian Scientist, as was my mother. The two of them would spend literally hours into the night discussing Mary Baker Eddy. Aunt Nell usually slept all day, arising at 6 p.m. in time for dinner, and having her regular daily massage therapist come to give her a treatment. Her breakfast was always a glass of sauerkraut juice. She was a robust, healthy woman who lived to be ninety-five.

As one of her many mentees, I was attempting to be a serious student despite the quality of my teachers, but Nell began worrying about my social life and chastised me for not going out and having fun. After all, I was only eighteen. When Jenny and I received an invitation to a cousin's engagement party on the East side of New York, Nell said, "Listen girls, I'll loan you each a mink coat if you'll accept that invitation." We did not know it at the time, but my mother had sold Aunt Nell a full-length mink coat years ago to pay for the college tuition of Butler, Jenny and me. It was the same splendid mink coat that had been given to our father in Spain, and Aunt Nell had made two short coats out of it, one for each of us. Speaking of Aunt Nell's incredible generosity, Mother had also sold one of the pairs of diamond earrings from Spain to Nell. Nell had diamond rings made from them for Jenny and me to be presented to us on our twenty-first birthdays. We fell for her bribe, and, wearing our "new" mink coats, we set out to attend the party.

At the party, I was chatting with a gentleman who was producing a play at the Bleeker Street Theatre (one of the first off-Broadway theatres in New York). I was being most impressive, sharing all the places I'd lived around the globe when he asked me what I thought of Strindberg. "I've never been there," I replied airily. "Strindberg is a playwright," a soft voice whispered over my right shoulder. I turned around and met Jim Macdonald.

Jim asked me to go out with him that night and I told him I couldn't go because I was going to the Amato Theatre. I didn't believe anyone in New York would really want to go to the Amato Theatre, which is a studio for aspiring singers who need to practice their operas. He surprised me by saying he'd like to go and I said, "If you really want to go, you can pick me up at 7," and he did.

We had three dates in a row after that and when I got home from the third date I told my sister, "Oh Jenny, I think I'm in love." On the fourth date, he gave me a package of tickets for one whole year ahead, for theatre, opera and dance performances. He knew the way to my heart. The thing about Jim was that he loved art and music and people – just like I did. He got both of his degrees from New York University – one in Aeronautical Engineering and the other in Public relations. He had grown up in Brooklyn, the son of a Presbyterian Minister who retired to Connecticut. We dated almost every night for a year and then we got married.

Rainbow's End

Our wedding ceremony took place at Fall Hill in May of 1950 (Jim and I never could remember the anniversary date and joked about it all of our married life – I still can't remember it). Jim's best man was Hugo Bartok, the Voice of America contact for the Hungarian Desk, and my sister, Jenny, was my Maid of Honor. Hugo and his wife, Alice, were Jim's best friends in New York.

Jim's father, the Rev. Peter Albert Macdonald, officiated. With Dad holding me firmly as we came down the stairs, we made a dramatic entrance at the landing and turned to take the last five steps into the wide central hall, where my parents had been married fifty years before, and where Jenny would be married three years later. Jim's mother, Adele, stood with the other guests in the hall, which had been built originally as a place for large gatherings.

The dress I wore was an exquisite antique gown of satin, pearls and lace that had been loaned to me by a dear friend, Penelope, who was soon to become my sister-in-law. The elegant full-length dress fell close to my body, with long sleeves and a modest neckline.

Speaking of modest, mother had two beautiful wedding cakes in the shape of hearts sitting side by side on our dining room table. One cake was for Bessie and the other for James. The minute I saw the cakes, I hated them because mother would not put one cake on top of the other. It was too sexually explicit. She was a prude who had not even told me about menstruation as a girl and considered sex a subject that was not to be mentioned in public. Two weeks prior to the wedding, she had come to New York to discuss final details with me and I told her I had a diaphragm fitted because I thought Jim and I should wait a while before we had children. She said, "Well, dear, let me take that back to Fall Hill and pack it with your trousseau."

Another example of Mother's prudishness was the incident that occurred three years after we got married. Jim and I went to visit Fall Hill for Christmas. It was our first visit home since the wedding and we took our best friends, Joe and Riley, a homosexual couple who also lived in a coldwater flat in the village. Mother gave them a room in the kitchen cottage which served as a guest house and she also put Jim there. She put me in my childhood room with my sister. Only her daughters knew what a prude she really was.

At the end of that visit, Jim had had enough of her interference and left a note on my bed that he and our friends were driving back to New York that morning and if I chose to join them, he would be delighted, and join them I did. We had a hard time talking about that for several days until I admitted that mother's hold on me was inordinately strong. It was to remain so forever, but that hold did not keep me from living a full life of my own.

Chapter 10
A Coldwater Flat in the Village

When we were married, Jim and I moved into his coldwater flat. My father cried when he first saw it, but then he held me in his arms and said, "Dear little Bessie, anywhere you are is the end of the rainbow." I knew why he cried. He had always provided such beautiful homes for me and our flat was far from beautiful, with the entrance up straight bare stairs that passed garbage cans at the front door. It was in the lowest part of Manhattan near the entrance to the Holland Tunnel on 50 Grand Street in Greenwich Village. Jim used to say, "We're in the lowest part of the city – morally, economically and geographically." I loved it.

Each landing in the stairwell had one bare bulb and dangling from the bulb were several wires that the tenants had connected to in order to siphon off some power. We were on the second floor and we actually had our own toilet. One day, the small bathroom cubicle filled with dust as plaster from above came through the air vent. It seems the tenants on the top floor were eliminating one of their walls to make a larger room. When the landlord found this out due to our complaint about the plaster dust, he nearly had an apoplectic fit. That young couple on the top floor were removing a sustaining wall.

In order to decorate the flat, my mother helped me with lovely things – a beautiful Chinese rug in blue and cream, antique Chinese figurines which we made pedestals for on the brick wall above the fireplace, and a stunning carved camphor trunk which served as coffee table and storage unit and added elegance to everything. As a wedding gift, a friend of Jim's had given us seventeen yards of beautiful yellow cotton and I spanned our floor to ceiling windows with this soft color. Jim's furniture from college was all bamboo and fit perfectly into the oriental décor.

Being a coldwater flat, the fireplace was a working and essential commodity. Our wood, which we burned in a Franklin stove (also from my mother) was gathered in the evening as we strolled around Chinatown, picking up crates and other packing debris.

Our friends were artists and painters and actors, many of them clients of Jim's. One of the artists, Tom Sullivan, did Jim's portrait and it hangs to this day in my daughter's home in Virginia. Jim was a quiet, thoughtful man – six feet one, blonde, blue-eyed and quite handsome. He had a beautiful Roman nose. He was slender, with long fingers and

Chapter 10: A Coldwater Flat in the Village

long limbs. He never gained any extra weight. He was well-read and so intelligent. He adored music and opera and art and we saw things through the same eyes.

We shared our food with our friends as they did with us – nobody had much money. I bought my groceries in a second hand shop – the one-day olds and the dented cans. We saved a lot that way, but we ate very well and we all offered our best to one another.

One day I made a chowder from the contents of a dented can and Jim and I both got a serious case of ptomaine poisoning. That was when I learned the lesson never to eat food from a dented can. But the consequences were even more serious than mild food poisoning. Jim and I were too sick that night to go to our small side jobs "supering" in operas (taking parts that did not require singing). We got $2 for rehearsal and $4 for performance, plus, for me, the delight of being on stage, back stage and behind the conductor's baton.

That night, we found two actor friends to substitute for us, and because they had not rehearsed, they led the street scene in La Boheme off stage into the wrong exit, where nobody fit, and Jim and I were fired … all consequences of a dented can!

That couple who substituted for us, Arlene and Bob Robison, took a flat above us after that fateful night, and became lifelong friends. The couple under us, Bob and Wanda Ramsey, on the first floor also became lifelong friends. They too were in theatre and Bob was a very talented and eventually successful set designer and director. In his career, he eventually designed for television sets and moved to Connecticut, but we never lost close contact. Bob's creativity showed up strongly in their apartment, as within the large kitchen, he created a walled dining room and put in a bath with a tub.

One day, Wanda was exasperated to find white dust constantly being deposited on the floor around her "dining room." On further inspection, to eliminate this problem, we were all together when we pulled some sheets

Rainbow's End

of straw matting off the wall and found it filled with little bugs. The matting had been collected some months before from the streets of Chinatown, marked hippopotamus skins. So he replaced his lovely living and dining room walls with something more conventional (and the hippopotamus skins burned nicely in the fireplace, bugs and all).

Wanda had been raised by her affluent family in Paris and her maiden name had been Galezofska – Polish/Jewish. She had come to America because her father had to get her out of France as the German threat to Jews accelerated and, tragically, resulted in the death of her mother, who was simply picked up and whisked away one terrible day in Wanda's 20th year. Her father had tried to hide his daughters, Wanda, 20 and Iza, 25, in the farmer's cottage at the gates of Chenonceau (one of the most exalted Chateau of the Loire), but later, decided it would be safer to send them to America. When the sisters came to America, they got a job in the bargain basement of Macy's (these elegant girls raised with silver spoons in their mouths now were polishing stainless steel flatware along with their English).

Wanda fell in love with Bob Ramsey after she applied for a job in the box office of the Bleeker Street Theatre where he was producing a play and for which Jim was doing publicity. Our friendship developed quickly because we met after every performance at about 11 p.m. and all had a late dinner together. Bob and Wanda married shortly after Jim and I did, so Bob's coldwater flat and Jim's coldwater flat were now filled with two wives who were dear friends. It was such joy for me to have a dear friend who understood a pampered life and when Wanda became pregnant the next year of her marriage, she hired a nanny there in the coldwater flat and had an English pram parked next to the garbage cans and they gave the nanny their bedroom – the only bedroom – and set up a room for themselves in the "dining room." When Wanda was pregnant, the crudely manufactured bathroom had such a narrow passage that Bob had to adjust the walls so Wanda could get through to the tub. They were the talk of the neighborhood.

As to the neighborhood, we were a family with everybody on the block. It was the Italian section of Greenwich Village. The store owner two doors down treated us like his children, pampering us, hovering over us, asking questions about our personal life, and simply adored the Ramsey's new baby boy, Greg, who was destined to one day become a successful director like his father.

Chapter 11: Aix en Provence

While walking with Wanda one day in our neighborhood, parading the beautiful baby in his pram, we overheard two mothers discussing their woes, lamenting that one of their daughters was getting married and moving uptown, out of the neighborhood, and they were so distraught. How could she!

Years later, when I went back to visit the neighborhood after the Ramseys, Robisons and the Macdonalds had all moved on to more affluent lives, I emerged from the subway stop in the evening and was walking towards my old flat when I heard more than one footstep behind me. I saw it was a menacing group of young men – a neighborhood gang who did not recognize me and were preparing to molest me. So, I picked up my speed and burst into the storekeeper's shop, and was quickly recognized and saved. Nothing like that ever happened when I lived there because I was part of the neighborhood. It was a little piece of Westside Story come to life.

Back to the jobs we once held while living in the Village, another side job for Jim and me was proof reading for the National Bureau of Economic Research, a tedious but nicely paid occupation which involved proof-reading the books written by an economist named Arthur Burns who later became the economic advisor to the president.

One of the most memorable jobs I had was as a super was in the opera, Aida, when I mimicked playing a harp as the orchestra actually played – and Radames and Aida sang their final love duet in the tomb below. Jim was the captain of the victorious army in that performance and had been issued tights by the costumer who would look at the height of the person, stretching the tights in each hand to see whether he got a long, medium or short pair of tights. He got a long, of course.

Speaking of operas, a notable opera was La Boheme, the very opera that Jim had taken me to when we first began courting, and when I saw tears in his eyes during the love duet, I had realized I loved this man.

Jim had put his aeronautical engineering degree in a drawer and gotten another degree in public relations. That's why we were in the Village. He was doing publicity for artists and actors and singers. Most of his clients became good friends, among them Elia Kazan and Bea Arthur, who went on to stardom, but waiting for the paycheck became impossible after three years. The Korean War had begun and Jim pulled out his degree and went off to Republic Aviation on Long Island to apply for a job. They welcomed him with open arms and soon, with more than that, because he was a very talented and good worker.

Rainbow's End

When Republic Aviation offered him the job in Aix en Provence, they questioned him about his wife and whether she might be able to adapt to life abroad. Jim had a wonderful Scottish quiet sense of humor and said nothing, but went with me for the interview. I was soon telling his boss what life in Aix en Provence would be like and offering to help any other Americans they were sending to adjust to the newness of it all.

Chapter 11
Aix en Provence

It was in my twenty-fifth year that I boarded the airplane with Jim and flew to Aix en Provence, France. It was 1955 and we were very excited because he was being sent to Aix to be an aeronautical engineer. He was to make pieces for exchange for NATO's F-84 Fighter plane, being manufactured in Etang de Berre.

As we were landing at the Marseilles Airport a voice in my head said, "I'm home." It thrilled me to see that countryside. It was so familiar that I felt, indeed, that I'd landed on my feet. I had lived overseas most of my life, after all, having spent only about seven years in the United States.

The first thing we did was check in to our hotel. I hardly dared put my foot to the ground it was so beautiful. A country hotel it was – red brick in fields of poppies – soft hills – and a Michelin Menu on the door saying that this was a one-star hotel (which meant we could look forward to peace, quality, and simple, exquisite food). Then, to top off the whole thing with extra ambrosia, we were led to a room on the second floor of a small cottage at the gate. Since it had been booked for an undetermined amount of time, the management decided to give us our own little villa! What could be more heavenly for almost-newlyweds?

In the hotel itself, Jim's boss had been booked with his wife and though he was fifty years old and his wife was forty-three, they, too, were newlyweds. He had waited for his bride since high school but she would not leave her mother until her mother died. Alice and Hugo were from Brooklyn, with an accent that went with it, and during the meal while ordering from the menu, I could see the restrained laughter from the waiters as Hugo tried to pronounce the French names. They became our dearest friends – not only during our time in Aix, but for years afterward. Alice and I spent our time during the day looking for a place to live. Housing was in extremely short supply. France and all the other European countries had not really recovered from the Second World War, so the places we looked at were most unusual.

Landlords loved to rent to Americans. They had found in their experience that we were dependable, paid the rent and very seldom trashed the place. Another plus was that we did not insist on a long lease. We would take what we could get. Even Republic Aviation didn't know how long we'd be there.

Rainbow's End

After six months, I found a perfect place. I was escorted by the Baron Guillibert de la Lauziere into his beautiful, roomy townhouse, which in Europe is more like a chateau than an American townhouse. The curved, balustraded stairs led up three floors and we were offered the middle floor as an apartment. The front hall was spacious and the living room was glorious with three tall French windows from ceiling to floor looking out over the garden. The Baron let us use his heirloom Louis the 15th Furniture, with tapestry created by his family over many generations in a series of scenes from Aesop's Fables. I added Vin Rose pink chintz drapes from ceiling to floor, which brought out all the beautiful colors of the tapestry. The Baron was delighted.

The second and third rooms were equally beautiful, but there was no kitchen, of course. The kitchen, for the original home, would have been in the basement. However, the Baron hoped that I would also hire his faithful servant who had walked in from the country every day for the past fifteen years that he had lived there. Ilodie, the servant, was five feet tall, wiry and strong, and I simply loved her. She and I created a kitchen out of the guest washroom. We put in a two-burner table top stove and a table and, for the next year, she helped me clean it up after my long French dinners. Cooking became my hobby while I lived in Aix.

I loved every part of French cooking. I became a Julia Childs. I went to French cooking school in Marseilles, taking a bus to Marseilles and then taking a trolley to the port, where I would buy the food the school had instructed us to bring. From the shore, I'd bargain for fresh fish with the vendors in their boats. They did not give you the fish filleted and scaled – we did that for ourselves. In the market nearby, I would buy a chicken freshly killed – handed to me by its legs – head down and plopped into a bag. The only vendor who offered you a bag was the man who sold the chickens. You had to bring your own shopping bag for everything else – that was a definite must. The fish were wrapped in a newspaper but the vegetables and bread were all handed to us as is.

I went to class once a week. There were about fourteen students. I was the only American and really had to prove myself. They would give me the nastiest jobs to see if I'd do it – cleaning the chicken and singeing his feathers; cleaning the octopus; filleting the fish … they seemed to keep the rinsing and chopping of vegetables to themselves. It surprised me one day, though, as they did the lettuce, that they would carefully cut out the center's stiff stem and keep only the soft leaves on either side of it. A French salad is just made of lovely fresh lettuce – more like the bib lettuce than iceberg – n fact, there was never anything like iceberg. Bib lettuce and a delicate French dressing followed the main course – to clear your palette for cheese or desert or both. Some other French traditions dealing with cuisine:

- Bread is never served with butter –bread is to clear the palette not to add to it.
- Salad always follows the main course
- Vegetables are often served separately as their own little course
- Sauces are the quintessential ingredient of French cooking
- The whole 1, 2, 3 star Michelin procedure is based on the quality of the sauces
- Sauces are an absolute sign of how good a cook you are. You keep leftovers of everything you cook – little bits of flavor to add to something else. You think of the sauce at all times.
- Béchamel sauce – white sauce – puddings – soufflés – milk and butter and flour – you must learn to make it smooth – then you've got the brown sauces – bits in the pan when you've fried your meat – add a little stock.
- Learn when to add wine – which is almost always.
- Before I left the school, I had to know how to make a soufflé – a bit touchy to make sure it climbs the wall of your dish.

At the end of the morning of cooking, which lasted about four hours, we would sit around an oval table and our master teacher – a woman - would place herself at the head and begin a critique of the meal. Shortly after lunch I'd walk back down to the trolley stop with my menu in hand for next week's shopping and make my way back to Aix for the hour ride.

With nothing else to do but learn French and learn the cuisine, I would shop again for my dinner with Jim and practice everything I'd learned. An American once asked us what we did with our time. I answered, "I shop and I cook."

Rainbow's End

Weekends, though, were a different thing. Jim and I bought ourselves Velo Solex (bicycles with a motor over the front wheel). The motor bikes weren't very powerful but they certainly helped over the miles of countryside as we explored the area around Aix. We found every little restaurant that we could think of to have lunch or dinner.

On one glorious outing, we had gone towards the mountain called St. Victoire (the one that Cezanne loved to paint and the one that was actually to become part of my view in our second home in Aix). Cezanne's home is on the outskirts of Aix and was a favorite tourist site. While we were pedaling the countryside on a perfect day (in Aix almost every day was a perfect day), we set out on a small road which was cut through acres of red poppies and lined with Sycamore trees as in the days of the Romans. If that wasn't like being in the Wizard of Oz, I don't know what is. We came to the little restaurant that we had read about – a beautiful terrace was laid out with a canopy of wisteria in bloom, and in the distance, we could see not only St. Victoire but Picasso's chateau. He was in residence, we'd heard, but tourists were not allowed, so we never got in.

As we sat on the terrace, we were first served a platter of Char Cuterie – cold cuts and vegetables. That's where I learned to put butter and a pinch of salt on each radish. There were little scallions scattered on the plate, tender and small from their garden, and two or three pates, locally made (pates were so various – some made with liver – or ground up meat of all kinds). A thin slice of Cornichon (tiny cucumber pickle) accompanied every bite of pate. There were tomatoes off the vine, too. This was followed by a beautifully grilled fish from the stream nearby – Truite Almondine – and then the heavier dish, Canard (duck), simmered in a stew with little potatoes and carrots and, of course, red wine. Salad came next, and then desert – usually cheese at first – then followed by a simple poached fruit.

The little restaurants and simple cafes we went to in the French countryside did not offer fancy deserts or fancy sauces – unlike the 3-star Michelin Restaurant called Beauregard that served seven deserts and was famous for its sauces. We had found it to be a long ride to get to Beauregard, with the roads crossing through farmer's fallow fields, heavily encrusted with iron spikes poking about two feet into the air for at least twenty miles. These were a World War II remnant of the resistance, trying to keep planes from landing, but Beauregard itself was magic. It was a ghost town and we climbed into it in the moonlight to reach the ruined castle. The restaurant was at the foot of the hills in the peaceful valley below. Jim put his camera on a tripod in order to

Chapter 11: Aix en Provence

take a photograph of the town with moonlight only. The picture is haunting and, lying on the boulders which were dug out to create a cistern for water for the town took us into an ancient atmosphere. We sat very still for at least half an hour, absorbing the spirit of the ghosts. When we left the hills at about 8 p.m. and made our way down the crumbling path to the restaurant, we welcomed our aperitif with enthusiasm and began our seven course meal. I could say it was memorable, but I don't remember what I ate, except that I know after the third dessert I said, "Oh, no, no, I can't possibly eat any more," and the Maitre de came over rather intrigued by this young American couple who loved French food, and convinced me that I would be sorry if I did not at least taste the next four desserts. And, of course, I did.

Back to the little countryside café, which was one of the first of many of our gastronomic and cultural pursuits, it was hard to leave the beautiful scent of wisteria that day as we departed with many waves from the staff, who delighted in our enthusiasm. As we pedaled away from the little restaurant, I glanced regretfully toward Picasso's chateau once again. I had read that he painted his bathtub and ceilings and floors and I really longed to see it all. It was a huge, glorious true French chateau surrounded by olive groves. Now, although we never saw Picasso in his home, we did see him very often at the bullfights. Jim and I loved to go to bullfights and Picasso was always in the first row. He looked exactly like his pictures and he always had a beautiful woman on his arm. He would get a graceful bow from the Matador. Picasso was the center of attention wherever he went.

The most exciting bullfight we attended was in the Roman arena in Nimes. Jim and I learned there was a fascinating pageantry about the bullfights – a formation for the bullfight dance routine. It would begin with the heralding of trumpets – then the picadors would enter on their horses, looking snobbish and elegant. It was all so foreign and exciting. Even though the known end was so gruesome, it was just like going to the opera.

Jim and I began to study the history of the matadors, who were usually from a poor family and had begun their career as a picador (low man on the totem pole in a bullfight since it is his job to spear the big muscle on the back of the bull's neck to weaken it prior to the fight). This spearing was done with a great deal of flourishing bravado to make it beautiful – and it was encouraged by the audience. Then the matador would enter with his cape and the bull would be cowering in the corner. The bull's attitude determined the length of the performance. Was he truly cowering or was he simply mad? The bull claimed an area of the bull ring as his – almost as though he had a mate there – and the matador would feel out where the bull's area was and pick his place to fight accordingly. He could tease and flash his cape and do his dance and make the bull attack. He was pretty sure of being fairly safe unless he came between the bull and his area, so it was up to the matador to study the bull and know how to proceed.

If the matador was gored, his picadors came running in to distract the bull and pull him off so that the matador could be taken to the hospital. The length of the bullfight depended upon the matador's skill. If he was very skilled, it might last quite a while before the final blow was dealt – a sword in the forehead of the bull. It was a great honor to be a picador or a matador. They were considered "damn" brave and they got "damn" rich, becoming heroes of the land. (The word "very" was replaced by "damn" in respect to Mark Twain's editing advice … and it is acknowledged that "damn" works just as well as "very" every time!)

The bullfights in Spain and Portugal were much different from those in France. In Spain it was inclined to be bloodier with a stronger emphasis upon the death of the bull – a deeper desire to have the bull die and the Matador win and become a hero. In Portugal they do not kill the bull in front of the audience – there is no sword in his forehead – they profess to be more humane. The subalternos (people who bring the bull down) jump on the bull's back, twist his tail and grab his horns, generally endangering their lives. There are about six of them on foot – no horse for them. They make more money than they've ever seen in their lives – but it is damn dangerous – the bull is pretty angry by then.

Other weekends we would explore Roman ruins. They were in evidence everywhere from the aqueducts to remnants of towns. Aix itself was founded by Romans and the beautiful fountains everywhere are natural springs – some are even hot. The loveliest are three or four in the center of the Cours Mirabeau and those fountains are from Roman times. They are the reason the city was established in the first place and called Aix, meaning water.

I felt I had my own personal fountain near the front door of my hotel de villa. It was named the Quatre Dauphine (four dolphins spouting that beautiful clear water into

Chapter 11: Aix en Provence

a basin). That was the first thing my maid, Ilodie, did every day – she would fill containers from the fountain for drinking or use in cooking. It was a daily ritual.

One trip we took was to Arles to see Van Gogh's asylum where he died and to see for ourselves the sunflowers that he painted so wildly. What I think attracted artists to the area of Aix was the unusual light that the dryness of Provence produces. I have not seen it anywhere else in the world in that intensity. In most other places, the light lasts about an hour at that magic time of sunset or sunrise, but in Aix, it could last all day. Within the first few months of arriving there, Jim and I both bought ourselves a small palette of watercolors and paper but found we did not have the talent to go with it. Little did I know that my daughter, Claire, would become a marvelous watercolorist and make up for the pain I felt when I discovered I did not have the talent to match my imagination.

One spring weekend we went to Monte Carlo to attend the Grand Prix car race. Jim found these incredibly great seats on the balcony at the famous S-curve. The famous racecar driver Sterling Moss was driving that day – a red Ferrari. I'd never been to a car race before and my mouth dropped open in absolute horror at the sound that was coming down the street. It was frightening! The little cars whipped by so fast that I thought they couldn't possibly stay on the road – then they disappeared into tunnels on the long stretch to the grand finale. It was too exciting for words!

We spent the night in Morte Carlo, with its underground passage from the lobby to the casino. We did some exploring, of course, and ran into some famous folks that night. I remember walking right behind Zsa Zsa Gabor and being disappointed at her lack of fastidiousness. She was there with one of her rich old husbands and I noticed that the back of her lovely white lace dress had a smear of makeup on the collar. She was supposed to be so perfect and beautiful, but she wasn't, after all! We also saw Winston Churchill. He was very old by then, but definitely the master of his group, dictating where everyone would go and what they would do. I was always a great admirer of his and am still grateful to him for the foresight he had in leading his country. I also had the privilege of being in England and attended his funeral later, where the streets were

Rainbow's End

lined with temporary fences to control the crowds and after the funeral, Jim took a memorable picture which showed the crowd already gone but socks, mittens, scarves, the occasional hat, all remnants of the crowd, hung on the pickets of the fence.

Later, continuing our archeological explorations, we found a Roman town being freshly excavated (recently discovered). It was exciting because they had uncovered these beautiful mosaic floors in remarkable condition – the designs still bright and unfaded, and the early excavations of the water system for baths and household water throughout the town – so sophisticated! Within four years, before we left Aix, they had excavated the whole town. Jim and I watched the excavation proceed whenever we could. A pottery was set up nearby and the clay was excellent – just as it had been for the Romans. We bought a Roman oil lamp – supposedly an artifact from that excavation. There was easy access to the ruins – they hadn't been invaded by tourists yet. They were simply digging and we were simply walking all around and over the ruins – nobody stopped us. As we walked, I imagined the whole town coming alive – walls went up in my mind, painted with great murals – something like Pompeii – the beautiful floors and the echoes of the market place seemed to resound as we walked around in the quiet. It was easy to create the town in my mind and be in it with the ghosts.

Jim and I were totally in sync. It turned out years later when he took a test for his abilities – the Johnson O'Connor test – that he would have scored highest as the head of an archeological team. Our interest in archeology led us to search for Antas, which are prehistoric homes built with huge boulders – usually into a hillside. The cavemen were aware of the benefits of building into the hills – the perfect temperature of it. There was a map that the French government produced to help us find these Antas. They could be anywhere – just off in fields where you wouldn't dream you would find anything. But if you came to them at the right angle, you would find the entrance. We went further in our studies and as the years went by, we found extraordinary caves in France, Spain and Portugal.

Because of our extensive searching, we came to an astounding discovery – the prehistoric cave of Lascaux, France – near the Pyranees. It had been discovered by two young boys who had fallen into a hole and found themselves in it. The second part was it was not yet open for heavy tourism so we saw it in pristine condition. We had gone to Lascaux especially for this search, staying overnight in the town in order to start out early in the morning to climb the hill to get to the cave. Our guide was one of the boys. It was

Chapter 11: Aix en Provence

a low ceilinged cave completely covered with drawings of prehistoric animals and the hunt. The curves of the cave had been used to give the animals three dimensions, much as Picasso's contribution to pottery when he used the curves of pottery to enhance the animals he carved on his pieces. I hyperventilated in the excitement of being surrounded by almost life-like bison, antelope, stick figure hunters holding spears, fingerprints from their hands dipped in paint and pressed on the wall. I felt the whole composition could have been created within my lifetime, and yet, here it was thousands of years old.

The cave was closed soon after we saw it, due to the destruction of the paint by the breath of the tourists. A second cave was found more recently and that one has been replicated. Only experts are allowed into the original Lascaux Cave.

Jim and I once went to Vence to see the Matisse Chapel. As we stood in the chapel, a few nuns came in – seeming to mimic his paintings on the walls – their black and white habits emphasizing the extraordinary religious awe of the place. The quiet was an essential element and made the stones seem to talk. We felt much the same feelings in every place we entered. Even while driving through the flower fields of the local perfume industry of Provence, there was a general reverence to the area that spoke of centuries gone by.

Meanwhile, back in Aix, the Baron was ready to sell his hotel de villa and we needed to find a new home. My maid, Ilodie, was the one who found it. She had been talking to her friend who was a plumber and had seen a lovely villa three miles outside of Aix, furnished and owned by an Englishman, Sir Clairmont Skrine, who wished to sell or would rent it to us while he looked for a buyer … once again, for an indeterminate amount of time. Sir Skrine was knighted because he had been the principal arranger between the British and American governments for the Shah of Iran's escape when his life was threatened.

We went out to see the villa and it was perfect. Large gates opened to lead me down to a slight incline where the four bedroom villa's spacious first floor dominated the two acres of vineyard. There was a small fountain in the front courtyard, a glassed-in vestibule as you entered (which I soon filled with pots of pink cyclamen and I painted the ceiling the same pink). Once again, the furniture was to my liking. Well-

Rainbow's End

made French Country Provincial – sturdy and handsome solid wood both in the dining room and living room. French doors, once again, out to the garden. It had a long kitchen with its own entrance to the yard and its herb plot – and four bedrooms upstairs. It had a two bedroom lean-to with its own entrance from the outside but a passage from the dining room through our coat closet into the gardener's living space. Now, I had not only Ilodie, the maid from the Baron, but I had a gardener courtesy of the landlord of the Villa.

Jim loved it as much as I did and we celebrated our moving in with a champagne party. The champagne bottles were cooled in our courtyard fountain and our guests were now both American and French, since our efforts at learning the language were coming along nicely.

The drama to this villa was that in 1958 DeGaulle was threatening to invade Algeria and the Algerians, who were fearful, were moving to Aix en Provence. Early in that time of threatened invasion, Jim was away and when he returned and found that I had not been aware of the possible invasion by DeGaulle (using Marseilles as a jumping off port), he was frightened and furious with me – a rare occurrence. He said, "Whenever I'm away, you must be aware of the current news and threats to your safety and always keep in touch with the consulate. Never ever leave yourself without knowing what is happening." So I never did again. I think in retrospect, I'm rather proud of the fact that he felt so sure that I would take care of things – that I would keep up with the news and do what was needed. He must have had a great deal of confidence in me, which is gratifying.

The mayor designated a large tract of land next to our villa for these refugee Algerians to build their own homes and bring their families. The fence between their land and ours was a fragile affair. The gardener and his wife restricted their daughter severely to cross the fence, as it would be extremely demeaning in their opinion for a French gardener's daughter to play with Algerian children, but the gardener's little daughter was quite a minx. The naughty little girl teased the Algerian children by throwing sticks and rocks over the fence to annoy them. One day, she hit one of the children on the head with a rock, causing him to bleed profusely and the Algerian women began trilling their high-pitched continuing distress cry as they marched towards my villa by the main road. The gardener and his wife immediately bolted their windows and doors and pulled their bratty daughter into the lean-to – claiming no responsibility for the incident. Jim was out of the country on business and I had to face the women alone. I managed to calm them down and convince them that their child would be alright and that I would swab his little

Chapter 12: London, England

wound every day with antiseptics and keep an eye on it until it healed. I simply told them I was qualified to do this. They could trust me, and they did, indeed.

The rest of the story happened a year later when the gates opened in anger once more but this time it was Charmasson, the gardener – red-eyed and terrified – holding a blunderbuss and accusing me of trying to kill him, and everybody else, too. I once again kept my cool, convinced him to sit down with a glass of ice water, and as he sipped, I called the gendarmes. They soon arrived and seemed familiar with Charmasson, and now I knew why the landlord from England had sent a telegram, when we rented the villa, saying "I suppose you know the problem with Charmasson." I had heard that he had an uneven temper but this was more than that. The poor man was schizophrenic and had shown no signs of it during the previous year. In fact, we'd had a very peaceful time with baskets of vegetables on our doorstep whenever they were ripe, bowls of grapes from our vineyard ready to make juice for my morning breakfast, and other delightful services.

Now that the gardener was gone, I was on my own in the garden. My efforts at growing Zinnias, however, were frustrated by something eating them during the night. A friend suggested I go out with a flashlight when it was dark and find out what it was. Lo and behold, it was large Bourguignon snails! So, I bought a snail basket and gathered snails nightly. I then hung the basket from a tree until their intestines were cleaned out. Then I would boil them, prepare them with butter and garlic, and eat them. That reduced the snail population effectively and my Zinnias began to bloom.

This was the villa where we could see St. Victoire from the terrace, but the delight of living there was coming to an end since Sir Clairmont, our landlord, could now sell the villa because he no longer had to provide equivalent quarters for the gardener (according to French law). The search was on for a new home and Ilodie once again found it for us back in the town.

It was a rather modern little house without much glamour, a big comedown in my opinion, but it had two lovely bedrooms and plenty of light. Once again, we hoped the second bedroom would accommodate our longed-for child.

We had been married for nine years and desiring a child all along. I had an excellent dressmaker in Aix and whenever I would get depressed about not being pregnant, I would have her make me a beautiful dress. I was known to be quite fashionable by this time, but the style of my wardrobe would soon be changing, due to the wonderful advent of maternity clothes.

An American friend working for Republic arrived. His wife was pregnant and she needed to find a doctor. They came to me, as they often did, to ask me to help her in the process of getting settled and speaking French. She asked me to go with her to all her doctor appointments in order to translate for her. The doctor she found was very sympathetic to my story of wishing I was pregnant and suggested that he examine me and my husband, as he had some expertise in that area. The result was that he upped Jim's testosterone by giving him some medication, found that I had a tipped uterus and advised us to follow the rhythm system in order to facilitate pregnancy, at least during my fertile period. It worked! Nine months later, I gave birth to Claire Elaine Macdonald, but not in Aix en Provence. By that time, we had been transferred by Republic to London, England.

It was an unexpected move. I was eight months pregnant when we were told we were to go to London. It reminded me vividly of my mother's experience of having to leave Barcelona, Spain at nine months pregnant with my youngest brother. Her move so late in her pregnancy was necessitated by a much more urgent cause, which was the safety of the family from the revolution, but it was one of the many parallels in our lives.

I was miserable about the move … having become so bonded with the culture, climate, beauty and people of Aix en Provence, and also having to leave my maid and my doctor, in whom I had such confidence. I did not look forward to the unknown. Jim and I were too young to object and only learned to do that in later years.

As we drove to England, I developed a cough. It turned into serious bronchitis which evolved into pneumonia. I coughed constantly.

Chapter 12
London, England

We booked into the hotel that Republic had prepared for us and I continued coughing constantly. All my ribs were sore, I was perpetually cold, I didn't have a home, I didn't know who would deliver my baby or where it would be born. I was at a low period of my life and I let myself wallow in self pity. As I was putting a tuppence into a gas fire in our room to keep warm, a doctor arrived, sent by the hotel. I climbed clumsily into bed, furious that I couldn't even see my feet. After examining me, he said, "My Dear," in a beautiful Scottish brogue, "you are coughing away your bairne and I will be getting you well soon." An angel had walked into my room – the first ray of hope that I had seen since arriving in London.

He found me a wonderful doctor who was assistant to the Queen no less. He was named Noel Goss, which means Christmas child. Mr. Goss (the higher up you go, you lose your doctor and become mister) had an opening for me in his clinic on my due date. I let God be back in charge. This episode in my life has always been strongly remembered every time I hear about refugees around the world. My heart is deeply stirred by their plight. Being homeless, for any human, is a tragic condition unequaled by any other.

The reason that Jim had been unable to find me a reservation at any hospital was because they thought he was simply taking advantage of the socialized medical system. Anyone arriving in the ninth month of pregnancy must certainly be using the system, in their opinion. But now, I had the Queen's doctor.

My few visits to Mr. Goss's clinic were unexpected, as he had his office in the first floor of his home on Harley Street (the posh street for doctors in London), and received me wearing a formal morning coat.

He booked me into the Princess Beatrice Clinic, where Claire (8 pounds 11 ounces) was born two weeks later on April 12, 1960. The morning of her birth was so thrilling and as Jim held Claire in awe, he said, "This is the best little do-it-yourself project we've ever made." I was cared for exquisitely there, staying in the clinic for ten lovely days. I was so happy to be a mother that I sang constantly and they put a sign on my door, "The Singing Mother." The care in the clinic was so personal and thoughtful of the mother ... the baby was in a crib next to my bed and only taken to the nursery at night, but brought to me for feeding. Nursing came easily to me and Claire was a perfect baby. If she did cry, however, there was an elderly nurse whose job was to do nothing but hold babies, and when she picked one up, it would snuggle into her neck and everything would be quiet. They taught me how to bathe my baby, how to nurse most effectively, and every morning before breakfast, I had to drink a bottle of stout to help with the milk (if only I had liked beer at that time). It's probably why Claire slept so well.

By the time my ten days were up, Jim had found a lovely apartment across the street from Kensington Gardens, where Princess Margaret's palace was, and our life as parents began. The first thing we wanted to do was try to keep as much of our freedom as we could, but the joy of caring for Claire began to make freedom less attractive.

Jim, as a father, interested me. He seemed to be in awe all the time. I thought that might be a temporary state, but actually, his ability to break down and just be a playmate never materialized. He remained an "in awe father" with all three children. He'd watch from a distance as I mothered and I have realized that his upbringing had everything to do with it. His father was sixty years old when he was born and his mother, forty. His maternal grandmother always lived with the family and was more the mother than his mother was, which gave him rather old parents. The loss of their first child, Lowell, at age twelve from a misdiagnosed ruptured appendix, had destroyed any youth that they may have retained. They even lost a second son, two months old, also from a misdiagnosed illness, and then they had the courage to give birth to Jim, but they never got over the sadness and never dared to absolutely love Jim the way they had their first son, Lowell. They lived in fear that Jim would die, and I think, not having ever experienced the vulnerability of joyful parenthood and only being raised in grief, Jim never seemed to hurdle that fear that his children were temporary. So, he held back on giving himself fully to his children, but that did not diminish his love. He cared for us beautifully and provided us with just about anything we wanted. The children may not have felt his love at times, as he was unable to express it.

Our second-floor apartment was high-ceilinged and cool with balconies overlooking Kensington Court, where I would sit for hours with Claire's cot and chat with neighbors as they went by. I didn't know then that it was an elegant "socially correct" place to live. The apartment was long and narrow, with two large bedrooms on the left, the living room on the right, followed by a kitchen that was so big that I bought a stool with wheels on it to roll around from counter to counter.

From my balcony, I remember watching Nubar Guilbenkin, son of one of the richest oil men in the world and a great philanthropist, arrive at his office in his notorious London cab that he privately owned. He had replaced the trimming with gold – two gold lamps on either side of the windshield – and his chauffeur wore a gold-braided cap. Guilbenkan, it was said, loved the space of a London cab and the ease of getting in and out. He always had a fresh orchid in his lapel. In later years, I was privileged to experience some of the philanthropy that his father had bestowed on Portugal. He had given the country an elaborate facility for the arts and we were able to enjoy marvelous performances in the City of Lisbon.

While sitting on the balcony, I made friends with my Chinese neighbor who owned a restaurant a block away. It was one of our favorite places to eat out and we would either choose his place or an Indian restaurant or a pub, as we were still longing for French cuisine. I had to let up on the cooking as childcare happily consumed my time. I tried to keep up the cooking, but shopping for meals was no fun anymore. The most convenient market was Harrods Department Store with their famous basement floor of fabulous merchandise, but children were discouraged – so English – and I had to park Claire's carriage in a special vestibule at the door for carriages and carry Claire.

Claire was in a Norwegian low baby carriage able to be converted into a carry cot with folding wheels so that she and I could travel with Jim on our explorations through England.

My housekeeper, Robert, was so good that he also became the best babysitter I've ever had in my life. We could walk to Albert Hall for concerts. Parenthood did not curtail our love for theatre, concert-going, or traveling to explore our new country. I did, however, take Claire with me in our carry cot if we went out to friend's homes. It was unconventional to bring your child and they always wondered why I didn't have a nanny. I wanted to do it myself. I'd waited nine years, after all.

Our walks in Kensington Gardens were dreamlike. The paths were solidly bordered by flowers and there was an area devoted to Alice in Wonderland with a beautiful statue bordered by all of her characters. There were lawns to sit on, a lake to watch boating, and I always carried a blanket to put on the ground so Claire could learn to crawl. I had also made a friend in the hospital, Jeannie, whose daughter was born the same day as Claire and who lived on the other side of the park. Her husband had recently been accepted in the House of Lords and she always wore a hat. She and I would meet every day in the park and our daughters would lie on their blankets and coo. There were certain paths we did not walk, which the nanny's reserved for themselves. They had their children in the English perambulators – high, well-sprung and wide – and the nannies were always in a crisp uniform and the children incredibly, beautifully decked out. I never saw one of them on the ground on a blanket.

The medical care following a birth in London was excellent and free and we mothers would go to our nearest clinic, designated by our location – and have our babies checked every week. At one visit, I was confused by a baby who howled in a high-pitched cry constantly, never stopping. I asked the nurse why that child was so persistent in crying and the nurse said, "My Dear, that is the child of a mother who was on drugs." It was the first time I had ever thought about drugs.

When Claire was eight months old, Jim and I decided to take a vacation in Bordeaux, France, and share a villa there with dear friends from Aix en Provence, the Muller-Feuga's. We bought our tickets, packed our bags and took off with no problems until we tried to return. We had neglected to get Claire any papers. We were detained at the airport until they were satisfied that we were her parents and not abducting a French child. It was much like the Solomon occasion of the mothers bringing the babies for King Solomon to decide who the real mother was. The security guard sitting in his high desk was much like a king sitting on his throne, and he made all of us feel very low class, saying to me in jest that he would have to keep the child overnight. I was much too upset to take the joke and burst into tears and said, "If she's going overnight, I'm going overnight." The guard quickly jumped down from his high pedestal and tried to make up for the mistaken jest. It probably had a lot to do with his finally accepting the fact that we were her true parents.

Claire was walking when we left London – about fifteen months later. We left to come back to America to Republic Aviation on Long Island once more. While in London, Jim had noticed the new technology of computers and how effective it was in business. He decided he wanted to get a degree in computer science. So, when Republic called us back to the center office on Long Island, Jim applied for a degree in computer science at his alma mater, New York University.

Chapter 13
Long Island & Back to England

We bought a small Cape Cod house in Northport, Long Island, with two wooded acres of land. It was a delight to Claire and me. We did not have Kensington Park, but we created our own Alice in Wonderland Park, bringing her dolls and making houses under rocks and playgrounds out of sticks, etc. Claire remembers those walks to this day and she attributes her ability to be an artist to the fact that I allowed her so much freedom to explore her imagination.

We put up a swing which Claire absolutely loved, and Jim designed a sandbox with high sides and a wonderful lid that covered the whole box and the strong hinges allowed you to open the lid so that it would become a slide. He put tin roofing material on the inside of the lid to make it the best slide ever. I wish he had patented it. Jim also put up an adult swing for me, as I loved to swing, too. I still have a swing in my yard today.

Jim continued his work with Republic, leaving the office in the afternoon and driving into the city to take his courses at NYU and driving home at about 11 at night. I took care of my child, did housekeeping, and volunteered as an assistant for a Montessori Nursery School where Claire was accepted happily. In that daily routine, I developed a desire to have a school like that of my own one day.

After two years, I became pregnant again and Kenneth James Macdonald was born on Long Island in a Jewish Hospital on April 13, 1963. I didn't care for the hospital. They circumcised him without asking me what I thought, which I resented, and they didn't let me have natural childbirth. I felt cheated of the experience, but Kenneth was healthy and Jim was thrilled to have a son. Once again, though, Jim was caught up in work and school, and I missed having household help. Both of us were unhappy and uncomfortable in America. It was and is the best country in the world, but not as easy to live in because of so many choices.

Rainbow's End

The blessing of my job was that both children were accepted at the school and, though Ken was put in a crib, he was part of the daily activities. Mrs. Muren, the owner of the school and the only teacher, used her own home as the school and had fifteen students in the morning and fifteen in the afternoon. She was wonderful. She made organic food for all the snacks and lunches. She attended to each child's personal needs. For example, one little boy was hyperactive. He would come in the door and rush out the back in order to play in the safe, fenced in yard. Mrs. Muren had tons of sand brought in every year to ensure the safety of all the falls. She insisted I let Ken climb up little ladders even when he could barely walk and simply made sure each child was given the activity they most needed. She had a patient, consistent ability to keep order. Children were taught to put away their toys when they finished in the pre-dedicated areas and cubicles; to put on their own coats; empty their shoes of sand before they came in, and help each other at the table with tasks like pouring the milk or helping smaller children cut their meat at lunch. I never did have a Montessori school, but I made sure to send my children to them when they were of age.

Recently, my sister, Jenny, took a marvelous photograph of mussels congregating on a dead branch floating in the quiet bayou – they grow in a cluster as if they love each other and want to stay in families – that's how they grow, in clumps, with each one trying to stay as close as possible to the other. When you pick them, they are definitely well-attached. Jenny's photograph reminded me of Long Island Bay, where the children and I spent many hours on the beach. The beach at Long Island Bay, whether in the heat of summer or the chill of winter, is divine. By September, the mussels have broken loose from their weirs and it was then that I walked with my children, carrying a large plastic tote bag and picking up loose ripe mussels as they washed up on the shore. We would fill the large tote bag with mussels and take them home. The children would help me scrub each wild, black, shiny bi-valve lined with mother of pearl, clamped tight like a clam or oyster. We'd have to pull off the beard and scrape the barnacles. The beard had to be pulled off – fine, hair-like tendons with which they had grasped the weir. This was tedious work and a little knife had to be employed which only I used. Then I would prepare a large pot in which I made the sauce – I would chop up a tomato and onion and two stalks of celery – lots of butter and a little bit of chicken broth and let that simmer until the vegetables were tender. Then I'd throw the clean mussels on top and clamp on a lid without stirring.

Chapter 14: Paris, France & Genoa, Italy

In five minutes of high heat, the steam pushed the lid up hard, I would go in and give it two or three good stirs – replace the lid and in no more than five minutes – depending on quantity, the mussels will have opened their valves exposing their delicious meat – the diners are at the table and ready – I dished them out ladles of mussels into a soup bowl then go back to thicken my juice a bit with flour, white wine and lemon juice (roux) when it's ready, pourable with a slight thickness to it, I serve each person some of that juice with a large piece of French bread – pour a glass of lemonade for the children and a glass of chilled white wine for me. The two would have a nap.

When Jim finally got his degree for computer programming, he was so talented that Republic Aviation was already using him to lecture their employees on computers. However, an offer from Mobile Oil to be their program systems manager was irresistible for us – for they promised to send us back to Europe. We sold our little house and our first post was back in London, but this time I decided to live in a country village rather than in town. Claire was five years old and Ken was two at the time. Claire went to a Scottish School where I had to find material to have a Scotch kilt made with the Macdonald plaid and Ken was entered into a Montessori Nursery School.

Our house in the country near Hampton Court was in the town of Esher and the gardens of Hampton Court were our daily walk. We had a furnished four bedroom house with a half acre lot near a good bus line – a lovely flower garden in the back and an easy train commute for Jim to go to London.

My shock the first week was the outcome of an invitation by my immediate neighbor to come to tea at four o'clock. My day had been hectic. I had to buy a car, sign papers for Claire's school, and came back for the tea ten minutes late. My neighbor answered my knock and said, stiffly, "Here in England, we're on time." She did not invite me in. Within a week, I learned that she was slightly unstable.

I hired an aux pair who came highly recommended by friends in Aix en Provence and I also had a busy summer with the oldest son of our friends, the Muller-Feuga's from Aix, who came to live with us for the summer to improve his English. His name was Arnaud and I asked a neighbor what she fed a teenager, as she had many children. Just bangers and mash (sausages and mashed potatoes), she said, but frankly, that did not go down very well with Arnaud. The teenager took care of his own groceries and didn't even ask to be driven to the grocery store. He ran everywhere. He had a knack for taking care of children, would play with Ken and Claire constantly, whirling them around the backyard in a wheelbarrow and playing at Hampton Court in the renowned maze. We missed him when he was gone. It's interesting to note that he became a marine biologist and went to school at Wood's Hole on the East Coast of the United States. When Arnaud left, I also lost the aux pair because the winter fog rolled into the house when you opened the front door and Christine decided English weather was not for her.

The maid I did get to help me was from the hotel where we had stayed upon arrival. We had become very friendly and when I called her to see if she wanted to become a live-in maid, she accepted with alacrity and stayed with us until we were transferred to Paris a year later.

Again, the Montessori nursery school where Ken attended had needed help. I had volunteered and also begun a correspondence course to become a Montessori teacher. I finished the course by the next year, but by then we were living in Paris and I never again had the opportunity to use my degree.

Chapter 14
Paris, France & Genoa, Italy

After Jim was transferred to Paris, we found an apartment in the 16th Arrondissement. The apartment complex had a marvelous center courtyard where my children could play and I entered Claire into the American School on the outskirts of Paris where their bus picked her up every morning and brought her home. I also found a wonderful Spanish maid whose mother worked in the same apartment complex. She helped with Ken. My apartment in Paris had a maid's room near the kitchen. The maid had a beautiful voice and when she washed the windows while standing on the balcony, she would sing and often her mother on the other balcony would sing, too. We residents felt they were our local canaries.

My landlady left me her exquisite Waterford Crystal to use. When I broke a beautiful crystal wine goblet and asked my landlady how I could replace it, she said, "Oh it was a purchase of youth – an "achat de jeanesse." – and it didn't matter. She did not expect it to last very long.

I explored Paris on foot, walking everywhere – usually with Ken in a little stroller. I don't know another city that lends itself so well to private exploration. On one of our expeditions, we went to see the tearing down of the famous marketplace called Les Halles (lais all) and were entertained, surprisingly, with a magnificent light projection onto glass of Picasso creating his famous Guernica. In black and white, three huge panels spanning 180 degrees, with Picasso running back and forth painting in controlled lines, we watched him appear and then disappear as the camera focused in and out on the process. Suddenly, we'd see a line of black and soon, his arm and body, always in motion. Then he would run to the other side to balance that line with another, taking him momentarily out of focus again. It felt as though the Civil War in Spain was going on right there and then.

That evening, Jim came to meet us at the restaurant next to Les Hall called Le Petit Cauchon famous for its entrée of pigs feet – glutinous and delicious – preceded by an appetizer of raclette (a cheese brought up close to the fire to melt and as it melts, scraped off and placed on a piece of bread and handed to the diner). Ken, of course, had fallen asleep in his stroller and, being France, there was no problem having a child in the

Rainbow's End

restaurant, which wasn't always the case in England. Claire was at home with my singing housekeeper.

A housekeeper in that apartment was necessary as there was daily shopping to do and the laundry was all done by hand. There was no dryer but an ingenious rack which lowered and raised with ropes as a sail on a ship with the laundry draped over it and pulled up to the twelve foot ceilings – the heat up there drying the clothes beautifully.

Claire's American school turned out to be a disaster. The first incident was that nobody paid attention to the fact that Claire did not get off the bus on the return home and I was left standing at the curb waiting for her as the bus went by. After frantic calls to the school, they said she had gotten on the bus and I said "but the bus did not stop and she did not get off." Thank God, a parent called about half an hour later to tell me that her daughter had brought Claire home at the end of the line, so I got in my car and went to get her.

That wasn't all. Another incident occurred when the school had a special talent day scheduled for parents to come and see what their children had been doing. It was an enormously important event and many fathers had to fly back from some business trip for the occasion. While I was at the school and watched the parents gathering, it was discovered that only those that had been told about the event by their children had the correct information. The written notices had the correct date, which was not the date on which we arrived. There were crying children, furious staff members, and a few belligerent parents, and as I went out the hall looking for the headmaster, I found him cringing under the staircase. He didn't last long at that school, of course, and the only solution I could think of for the few months that Claire had to stay there was to volunteer to get on the bus in the morning and evening, chaperoning the children as they were transported. I got some other parents to take turns with me, but the school itself was not ready to take on that responsibility.

Within a year, we were transferred to Nervi, Italy, just east of Genoa on the Via Apia along the Coast. We found a heavenly villa owned by a sea captain. It was also furnished, with 90% built in furniture. It was particularly enjoyable as each floor had a full balcony and all the windows faced the sea. The back of the house was tucked into the hills. The children had frequent opportunities to walk down to the clear Mediterranean and swim, and they loved roller skating on the balconies – it made up for an American backyard as far as having a place to play.

Chapter 14: *Paris, France & Genoa, Italy*

Because of the villa's location, we not only swam in the sea, but picnicked on the hills above. In the right season, our housekeeper, Rosa, would go with us and help us choose wild mushrooms which she would pickle, and we would pick fantastic persimmons, each about five inches across, and bring them home to the delight of all our friends. One day, when we were at the beach, Jim asked a local fisherman for permission to borrow his motor boat and, with a picnic lunch, we tooled across the bay between us and Portofino. We stayed on this windward side almost a whole day, climbing over the rugged pits and ocean-made ponds and basking in the sun while the children discovered all manner of small animals and fauna in the crevices.

The other side of Portofino Rock, where we did not go that day, was where the famous town of Portofino snuggled. We did explore that town later on by car and it is truly enchanting, the little houses all painted in pastel colors and the protected bay a haven of tranquility for local residents, safe from the wild storms of the Mediterranean. There was one intriguing home, however, that did not fit this description. All we could see was about three hundred feet of a staircase from a boat landing at the water level into a mysterious gate, and a few windows showing that a home was, indeed, up there. We were told it was the home of Elizabeth Taylor and Richard Burton. They were said to have had many a wild argument there.

Our garden was masterful. It was on four terraces, as life anywhere in Genoa is up or down. The gardener was my employee and, again, I could not have rented unless I employed him, but he at least did not live in my house or carry a blunderbuss. He took perfect care of the plants and one hour and a half of my signing the lease was taken up with going over every plant to be sure that when I got it, it was in good health. The plants had come from all over the world. At the front door was a Bird of Paradise bush, which

Rainbow's End

I waited eagerly to see in bloom, but as the time came, each bloom was covered with a brown paper bag to prevent any strange pollination with the exotic plants from all over the world. The espaliered lemon trees (trimmed to shape) flanked the fifteen foot wall and every plant was treasured. The gardener was very fond of my children and enjoyed having them with him as he tended the plants.

Claire, Jim and I began taking Italian lessons upon arrival and within three months, Claire was ready to enter an Italian School. We could walk to Claire's school every day on a winding path which led straight above the villa. I have a picture of Claire, age 6, wearing her new uniform for the Italian school, standing in front of the lemon trees. Her "uniform" was a navy blue smock with a ridiculously large Navy blue bow at the neck. I had bought the bow when I told the store she was in the first grade. I was mistaken – the bow should have been white.

My little girl arrived new and different from the first day, but that only led to a very fortunate meeting with another mother whose daughter was also attending her first day of school. This mother was an Italian and she decided to take us under her wing. Her daughter, Lorella, and mine became the closest of friends for the rest of our stay in Italy. Even after we were transferred to Portugal, Lorella came to spend the summer with us.

At the villa, I enjoyed sitting on our large patio, separate from the balconies, and located in the garden. With my binoculars, I would scan the Mediterranean Sea and, once in a while, even my neighbors down below (until one day I saw another pair of binoculars from a second story room staring back at me.) After that, I focused totally on the sea.

One day, while watching the entrance to the Harbor of Genoa, I saw about ten oil tankers all anchored, waiting to be serviced in that enormous, well-equipped port. A feeling of ominous fear engulfed me at the sight of this armada of oil ships. This feeling of gut-gripping fear was uncomfortably familiar. I had felt it while at an outdoor performance of the opera Carmen in France when the gypsies came winding down a hill with their lanterns. At that time, I had looked at Jim and said, "Why am I afraid?" He had no explanation.

Some years later, when we were snorkeling in the Caribbean and I found myself swimming with a large school of fish that seemed to be following me, I experienced the same feeling of panic. They looked like barracuda to me and kept up the same pace as I did when I tried to swim away from them. These unexplained panic attacks disturbed me, but it wasn't until years later when I was in my fifties and consulting a therapist

Chapter 14: Paris, France & Genoa, Italy

on several unresolved issues that I discovered why a group of oil tankers, a gaggle of gypsies and a school of fish inspired fear in me. It seems that it came from memories of my early childhood in Amoy, China when I looked back from the rickshaw and saw a stream of lights being carried by bandits on foot preparing to attack our villa. That line of lights coming down a hill cemented my lifelong panic at the sight of any unified group approaching me. It had happened at parades, halftimes, baseball games, and at on-stage performances where groups gathered, and now I knew why.

My live-in housekeeper, Rosa, simply adored my family. She had been a Hungarian prisoner of war under the Nazis and she had the tattooed number on her arm to prove it. She had gone into the concentration camp as a young girl and come out as an old woman. I saw pictures of her and couldn't believe the transformation. About two months before we were moved from Italy to Portugal, Rosa started showing signs of depression. I would find her sitting on her chair in the kitchen oblivious to time, with the meal not quite finished or the beds not made.

One day, I had a houseguest – my friend Maitee Muller-Feuga, a French friend with a German name. In the morning, my friend Maitee walked Claire to school for me while I went to town to do errands in town. I came back to find her waiting at the front gate. My housekeeper had locked her out of the house because she thought she was German. The horrors of her past were enveloping her, too.

This brings up another parallel in the lives of my mother and me. Having experienced a gardener with a blunderbuss and a depressed housekeeper with a locking key, I was reminded of the serious incident with the consulate staff that my mother had to deal with in China with her number one house boy being revealed as a spy.

During our stay in Italy, Claire had emergency appendicitis. She was six years old and in first grade at the time, and Jim was away as he always seemed to be during an emergency. I was advised to take her immediately to the children's hospital which was, fortunately, not more than a few miles away towards Genoa. I drove Claire in our Fiat and left Ken with Rosa, and the gardener, who was wringing his hands in anxiety. Claire's stomach ache was so severe that she was quickly examined and admitted and the staff at the emergency room confirmed that she was having an appendicitis attack. They let me stay with her for twenty-four hours and then their policy was no parents and they sent me home. At least I had the first night with her –the first twelve hours after surgery – but the separation was agonizing. Later I heard from Claire that though she was well cared for, they examined her on a cold steel table – with nothing on – and all these strange people standing around her giving their opinion. The surgeon told me that Claire's removed appendix showed scars from four other milder attacks in the past, and now we knew why she so often had terrible stomach aches which we had assumed were from the stress of moving. After all, this was the fourth country for a little girl who was just six years old.

As to Jim being away during every emergency, there was a time when my third child, Lisa, had nearly bitten off her tongue when she fell while climbing at Fall Hill at age two, that Jim was actually there. I remember feeling how wonderful it was to have him by my side during a crisis. We went together to the emergency room at Mary Washington Hospital and they took Lisa into the examining room and we parents followed. They wrapped her in a papoose-like gown (meaning it strapped down her arms and tied them around her) put her on the table of the surgery room and announced they were going to stitch her tongue up and that anesthesia would not be used as it would cause as much pain as the needle stitching her tongue, I was appalled but had had the experience in Italy with Claire and knew the lifelong effect of treatment like that and when they told me that parents would have to leave the room, my dear husband said, "Alright, I'll leave, but you aren't going to get her to leave – give me the papers to sign and she will stay in this room or you don't do the surgery." They did let me stay and I stood against the wall promising them that I would not faint and if I did, leave me there, and I sang to Lisa all the time, "All around the mulberry bush, the monkey chased the weasel," over and over again. That child did not even cry

Meanwhile, back in Italy, while Claire was in the hospital, her Siamese cat which we'd brought from Paris was pounced on and killed by the neighbor's German Shepherd dog. Our gardener who was also gardener for the neighbor with the dog insisted that the cat be replaced by a kitten and that it be Siamese and it was the least the neighbor could do. Now, finding a Siamese cat in Italy is not such an easy thing, but the task was accomplished and the new kitten was in a basket with an array of toys to greet Claire when she got home after ten days. Claire cried, nevertheless, of course, for the loss of her cat. I remember both of us sitting on the floor with the kitten just crying – but it did go a long way to help ease the pain. The gardener buried the attacked cat in the garden and promised he would always take care of the grave. We all got together and made a real ceremony of burying the cat, with flowers and all.

Chapter 15: *First Time in Lisbon, Portugal*

A reflection of that experience was relived many years later when I took a trip to Africa to visit my very close friend, Kathleen Walsh, the wife of a foreign service officer. I was sitting in her walled-in garden on the day of arrival waiting for her to run some errands when I saw their gardener weeding a small grave. I went over to ask him about it. They speak French in Cameroon, and he said it was the grave of a cat owned by a past resident. He had promised to always take care of it, so I guess our cats are in heaven for sure.

After Claire had recovered from her appendicitis, I decided to take her to La Scala, Milan, to experience an opera. She and I went alone. Jim and Ken and the staff remained at the house, and she remembers it to this day. What she doesn't remember is that after driving home those many miles and parking in our garage at the bottom level of our terraced garden, she was so sleepy that I had to carry her all the way up to the house and I barely made it. It was worth every moment. She still loves opera, as I do. Last year, my sister, her Aunt Jenny, gave her season tickets to the Kennedy Center, which Claire can commute to easily from her home in Silver Spring, Maryland. The tickets were renewed for this year and Claire calls and tells me about each performance with such delight, so we are still enjoying the opera together. Speaking of opera, Jim and I had season tickets to the opera in Genoa during our time there.

Our life in Italy was comfortable. Rosa was a fabulous cook – both Hungarian and Italian food – and our new friends – both Italian and American – soon learned that Rosa was our cook and were anxious to accept any invitations for dinner – we became very popular. Her Hungarian Baklava, by the way, was a sight to behold. She would roll out the pastry thin – so thin you could see the pattern of the marble table through it. The pastry would cover the whole table and

Rainbow's End

she would sprinkling walnuts and honey and then another layer of thin pastry and repeat again, then cut into squares and finally the crispy many-layered ambrosia – confection was shared by our friends never to be equaled by any baklava that I have ever had. In other main course dishes, the amount of parmesan cheese that she would consume cooking in that kitchen was frightening, but I never put a limit on her grocery bill and we profited enormously by that decision.

Leaving Italy was not a traumatic problem for me because we had had two homes in succession only one year in each, and I had not built up any close friendships. All of the company we'd had in Italy were from Ohio, Canada, Virginia, couples from England and France, and elsewhere. Give them a guest room on the Riviera outside of Genoa and they flocked in. One other wonderful thing was that Jim had already found a home for us before we got to Portugal, so we didn't have to go to a hotel and that was enormous (a hotel always felt like a homeless situation to me).

Claire was seven and Ken was four when Mobile Oil assigned Jim to Lisbon, Portugal.

Chapter 15
First Time in Lisbon, Portugal

Jim had tried to describe the home for me and had said he hoped I'd like it. When we arrived at the front gate, I gasped in delight. It was the most beautiful home we'd ever had, even outdoing the Italian villa.

The neighborhood was made up of one acre lots and it was so pretty that the tourists were taken around it on their explorations of Portugal. The town was called Estoril and is about 25 miles from Lisbon on the coast. The garden was surrounded by hedges, trees, and walls, as our neighbors were. As I walked into the house, was thrilled to find myself in a large foyer with black and white marble floor, and a circular stairway to the second floor balcony. There were four bedrooms and a large master bath (which was an astonishing addition in Portugal where baths were usually extremely utilitarian). From the foyer downstairs, you walked into a beautifully French-doored living room with a fireplace, an archway to the dining room (also with French doors), and then to a patio. The owner had left only his crystal chandelier and large dining room table. We were delighted because this was the first home we'd have to furnish in Europe. From the dining room, you walked into a long hall (called a butler's kitchen, which held all the cupboards holding the china, etc.) and then into the well-equipped kitchen. From the kitchen, there was a wing for the maid's room and bath. The basement, too, was large, with washtubs, but no washing machine. My maid did all the laundry by hand.

On the first day, two ladies knocked on my door and asked to be my servants. After talking with them for a while, I did hire them and found out later that they had left a neighbor's employ and I was very sorry about having robbed her of her servants. It turned out that most Americans had the same experience of maids preferring to work for us rather than the Portuguese. After all, we didn't expect them to work on Sunday; we usually gave them a vacation in the year and we usually paid them more. So, we were undermining the economy unknowingly. They loved me.

We started our Portuguese lessons immediately and my teacher was a fairly young girl who turned out to be a wonderful babysitter as well. So, our Portuguese lessons turned into play-days on the beach and visits to a larger than Olympian swimming pool in the local grand hotel. The deep pool had seven diving boards and we watched skilled

Rainbow's End

divers in awe. Claire learned to dive at that pool and Jim and I practically had to hide behind each other in anxiety as she learned to dive from the lowest to almost the highest diving board. She was a beautiful swimmer.

There were many sights to explore there – a fabulous antique carriage museum, a small palace, an incredible castle in Sintra (a town in the hills about fifteen miles away) and another town called Obidos about 200 miles north, with an enchanting castle which was equipped to be a Pousada (Portuguese Inn run by the government).

There were frequent festivals in the streets. I think they must have celebrated every Saints day with something – bonfires, dancing to the scent of roasting fresh sardines (ubiquitous at that time – I'm told now that the sardine harvest off the coast of Portugal is grimly depleted). Jim and the kids and I jumped the fires and danced with them all and ate the sardines with our fingers just like they did. How to eat a sardine: you hold the tail up in the air, bend your neck left, bend your neck sideways, and nibble the meat off the bone – no tools required, and then throw the bone to the waiting dogs. Portuguese dogs are trained not to choke on bones, or so it seems. There are packs of wild dogs everywhere – not dangerous – simply looking for food.

Another town near us that tourists loved was called Cascais. It's a picturesque fishing town and the ships that go to the water off Cape Cod in the winter to fish for cod are extraordinary three-masted schooners. A memory I have of them leaving one morning in the fog with their sails raised, hoping for wind, creeping along, remains with me. I felt an admiration for them as I knew that they would be gone for six to nine months and come back loaded with cod, the staple fish for Portugal. They cook cod in over 100 ways and I never discovered one of those ways that appealed to me.

Now there was the important business of placing my children in the English/Portuguese School which was in the town of Carcavelos – only about five miles towards Lisbon from Estoril, also on the shore. It was nice for Claire to go back to an English speaking school. It was Ken's first real school at age four. I drove them every day and would pick them up. I have discovered in my years of parenthood that those hours immediately before taking your children and immediately after picking them up are the ones where they are willing to chatter about what's going on. It's an issue I have with them riding the bus. I think it would make a huge difference in the school system if we all had to take our children to school – the commitment would become bigger and more demanding and

Chapter 15: First Time in Lisbon, Portugal

we would find out much more about what our children do in school. Carpooling, too, is an incredible resource and children are also very informative when they're in your car with their friends. I consider that, too, an alternative to the school bus.

Claire and Ken adjusted very well to their school. Little Ken said, one day, Mommy don't ever be late when you pick me up. Why, said I "Because they'll leave me all alone out on the street and nobody will be there with me – that's what they said." As it happened one day, I got lost while trying to get back to Carcavelos to pick him up (he had different hours from Claire). I found myself near the Lisbon airport, a long way from my goal, and decided to go to the information booth in the airport and call the school. I could not get anyone's attention at the information  booth and I took my purse and whammed it on the desk in absolute exasperation and anger and started to cry. Immediately, two people came up to help me. Though they did not speak English, I managed with my haltering Portuguese to tell them the problem and to ask them to please call the school for me. That crying technique worked well many years later after Jim died when I was forced to leave Claire at a facility to recover from bulimia. I was going out their front door, crying, and the attendant said, "Oh, don't cry," and I once again turned around, whammed my purse on the wall of the hall where I was standing waiting to go out the locked door, and said, "If a mother can't cry now, when can she cry?"

Meanwhile, back in Portugal, Claire, one day, was sent home with a suspension notice and she said, "They say that I stopped up the sink in the teacher's bathroom and left the water on purpose to flood the school." Someone had told the head master that it was a girl with long hair down to her waist, which was what Claire had, though she was not the only girl with long hair to her waist. When I asked Claire if she had done it, she said, adamantly, "No!" So I marched back to school with the suspension notice in my hand and demanded to see the headmaster privately. When I told him that Claire did not do it, he said, "How do you know?" I answered, "Because she said she didn't." "Oh," he said, "All children lie." I answered, "Maybe yours do, but mine don't, so please look into this further because it's not Claire who did it." By the next day, another child confessed to the prank.

Those four years in the house in Estoril were almost as wonderful as life in Aix en Provence. The added wonder was to travel with the observations of our children adding to our own. Our son would find sea life in little puddles on the shore or notice how the anemones clung to the rocks in different patterns. We were always down at the beach just a block from the house and in Portugal the beaches are better for sand playing than for cold swimming. The tourist office says little about it, but it's a cold country with a hot sun. If the sun wasn't shining, it was chilly – I never remember being too hot.

Claire made two very close friends and spent most of her time with them. They lived in our neighborhood so that her after school hours were as happy as her school hours. We were very close friends with their parents, whose younger son became my son's best friend. He was a little red-headed boy named Guy – and the boys spent most of their time in our garden where they could climb the big trees, build a tree house, enjoy our rope swing, and also enjoy walking on the one wall between our house and that of our neighbor who was the son of Nobel, the inventor of dynamite. He was very friendly and didn't mind the boys peering into his yard. That was a big thing over there – the walls meant stay out.

You might remember that I mentioned that I was interviewed to see if I was capable of living abroad when Jim was first sent to Aix en Provence by Republic. When Jim was hired by Mobile Oil, the same issue came up and I convinced them again that I could be a savvy European wife and would help other Americans. Within a week of arriving in Portugal, not yet knowing the language, a couple arrived on my doorstep who had just been transferred there by Mobile Oil. She needed help with everything – not a good contestant for the job was my summation, but I put her on to a real estate agent who could speak English and perhaps find her a home with her requirements and offered to keep her three children for the day while she house hunted. That was a drastic mistake. They were brats and on their own decided to run around my neighborhood and ring the doorbells just for fun. Dogs were barking, maids were mad, housewives were indignant, and I soon learned about it. It took me weeks to go around and personally apologize to the neighbors. I only learned about it when my children told me after the three brats went home.

We had one more encounter with that unfortunate family who never found a home they liked. We met them the entire family at a bullfight one day. Jim and I never brought our children to the bullfights, but they had brought theirs and they were three rows ahead of us. The mother and father were arguing loudly in a violent marital dispute as the children, quiet for once, tried to make themselves invisible.

Later when I talked to the real estate agent about whether she'd found a house for them, she said, "Oh, Mrs. Macdonald, I can't possibly find a house that will suit that wife. She wants all the modern conveniences including a dryer (she was appalled at that). Soon after that Mobile Oil sent them back to Rochester, New York.

Our own life was idyllic. The two maids that I hired were simply wonderful. One did all the cooking and shopping and the other the daily cleaning and laundry by hand. It left me free to do many things I had wanted to do. I joined a lively English speaking book club, hosted many parties for Jim, was active in the children's school, and, of course, driving back and forth to school to pick up the children on different schedules took quite a bit of my time. There was no end of things to see and do in those towns along the coast, and shopping in Lisbon was simply delightful but very time-consuming. There was one department store and all the other shops were single item shops. Even to go for buttons would take an hour. Our clothes were made at home by a seamstress who came regularly, so I would need to shop for materials and trimmings, etc.

Just to give my reader an idea of the intricacies … one small street was nothing but button shops. I usually went with a friend, as leaving the children home with those two delightful maids was never a problem for me. They loved nothing more than to play with the children. One of the recent conversations I had with my son was surprising to me. He remembered experiencing terror in those early years in Portugal when I did leave him with those maids. He thought I'd abandoned him. I was completely unaware at the time of his insecurities – he seemed so happy with the maids. In retrospect, after thinking about what he told me, I know now that taking my children to a new country, a new culture, and into a new language and then assuming they would be comfortable was an appalling oversight. Leaving the children with the housekeeper while going shopping was something I considered the norm, just as it had been in my childhood. I see in myself now a huge ability to empathize that was not present in those days.

Another unusual "norm" was having a seamstress, which was what was done from Aix en Provence on. In Portugal, one of the first priorities was stealing a seamstress from someone else. I loved shopping for material and accessories. I had a dress made every few months for myself. We could buy bathing suits and underwear in the department store.

The "last" a measurement in European shoes was different from the American foot, somehow. I remember I could buy a Bali – Swiss shoe – that would fit. We had shoes sent from America. For my children, I would draw their foot on a supplied pattern board that Bass Shoes would send, and the children and Jim would buy their shoes from Bass.

Once, on a trip back to America for vacation I went shopping in New York with my dear friend, Wanda, from the days in the Village. We went to Macy's together as I wanted to buy "those new American sheets that don't require ironing." In the linen department, I almost wept at the confusion of choices. I asked Wanda to pick out the sheets for me. It's easy to forget American abundance.

Going out for lunch on a weekend in Portugal was a family treat. Anywhere you take children in Portugal becomes a happy affair. They love children. Our favorite restaurant was three miles west of Estoril. It had its own lobsters underneath the restaurant among the natural cliffs. It was outstanding. You would go down to that "basement" (a peephole to the sea beneath their building) and point out your lobsters. Their diver would go down and get the fresh lobsters, which would be cooked immediately and every diner wrapped in a big bib for the feast. The wooden mallets were already in place at every table. One day as we were about to leave, I turned around to leave a tip on the table and saw a gentleman's jacket at the next table covered with the splashing from Ken's hammering of his lobster. Instead of mentioning it to the gentleman I asked the waitress to please tell him when he was about to leave that I had left enough money for him to have his coat cleaned and would he please accept it with our apologies. I was too embarrassed to face the music.

On one of our weekend trips with visitors to go to see the castle in Sintra, we decided to hire the horse and wagon that was available and let it take us up the twisting road to the castle. It was a wonderful slow way to enjoy the countryside, but Claire wouldn't get in. She said it was too much for the horse to carry us all. When I told the

Chapter 16: *Return to Paris*

driver we weren't going to go, he was dismayed. He needed the income. My solution was to buy a bag of carrots at the nearby market and hand them to Claire to give to the horse and she accepted that as a solution. The driver was so relieved to have customers.

Jim and I took a trip without the children one time to Coimbra in the north of Portugal, a town devoted to academic pursuits, with a marvelous university where the students all wore flowing dark capes. The town looked like a city of birds and, as we sat in the café eavesdropping (something I love to do) we heard serious discussions on the philosophy of life. This was, indeed, a true university town with the whole town involved in learning. We visited the Joanina Library, built in the 18th century, and the minute we walked in, the feeling that knowledge was everywhere engulfed you, the quiet was palpable and the stacks of books must have been, as I remember, about twenty feet high, with balconies around and rolling ladders to access the books. The aura of light that one stood in came from small rooms all around the sides, each with a window, a chair and a desk, where the reader could take his book and explore. It was more a religious experience than an intellectual one.

Port wine is the major product of the region, but we didn't over-imbibe, and brought home quite a few bottles to share with our friends. I remember the deeply carved façade of the Cathedral of Se Nova, and the rest of our days were spent finding even more evidence of the incredibly rich and fluctuating history of that area, both in politics and religion. If I were a student, that's where I would like to study.

We were all speaking Portuguese pretty nicely after about five months. It was, however, necessary to have the children take lessons at home as well since the English/Portuguese school did nothing to integrate the students and kept them effectively separated even at recess time by putting the Portuguese segment in a separate building … so much for the English/Portuguese School. The English education, however, was good.

Another hobby I took on while living there was to tutor children with learning disabilities. It came about because a neighbor asked me and I was so intrigued at the possibility of helping her child and so strengthened by her faith in me that I subscribed for a course from Holland on teaching learning disabilities. This seven year old had been tested in their home country of Holland and given exercises and reading substitute exercises to do to help with his disability. It was a bigger job than the mother could handle and out of the blue, she had asked me to be the teacher. It must have been a God-given thing because I took to it like a fish to water. I wrote for more books to America on how to teach learning disabled children. I had a cousin whose son needed help and she knew which books would be effective. My success as a tutor with that first child led to two more students and became my passion. It was thrilling to invent exercises to overcome their obstacles in thinking.

Two examples: One little boy hated math of any kind – or any number – so we spent our hour in the kitchen cooking – making cakes and cookies – measuring the ingredients. As soon as he saw the reason for the numbers, he excelled. This was the Dutch child who, I've been told, grew up to have a bakery in Holland. Another child's obstacle was holding still long enough to listen and he could not seem to shape letters when he wrote. He just didn't like to slow down enough to take the time. We would go off to the beach and I would have him write the letters by making tracks as he ran on the sand. He delighted in leaving all kinds of messages for people who followed us. It was not a big step after that to get his hand to put it on paper. Once he got that transition under his belt, he too excelled. And so it went. I was re-patterning their brains at that time, though I didn't know it. Now, it's a well-recognized practice. I carried that ability into tutoring children in Fredericksburg, Virginia many years later, when Jim and I lived there.

In our American book club, someone was needed to help choose books for our monthly sharing and to write to England to the publishing house where we purchased the books. After three years of doing this, the assistant editor at the publishing house and I had shared many informative letters about books and life in general and when I did go to London to live, which I had not expected to do, I looked him up and we had a pleasant, lively conversation about choosing books for Americans abroad. Now, with neighbors nearby who usually spoke English quite well, a lot of other school mothers, and Jim's wide circle of colleagues at Mobile, my social life was busy. I even joined a French club to keep up my French.

Our family did experience a horrific earthquake while living in Estoril. It was reminiscent of the 1755 Earthquake which all Lisbonites constantly remember and live with – that earthquake causing the whole lower part of the city of Lisbon to be completely washed out. Lisbon rises from a flat plateau on the edge of the Tagus River to its beautiful heights, which lends the city a dramatic placement. The old town on the plateau was completely destroyed, so all that part is "new" since the earthquake of 1755, which is

Chapter 16: Return to Paris

talked about as if it happened yesterday. It was in 1969 that I was sleeping in my home in Estoril when I heard a profoundly deep, long rumble like the sound of an army shooting their handguns. It woke Claire and me up, but not Kenneth, who was in his room recovering from bronchitis. Unfortunately, Jim was away on a business trip, and it took me about two minutes before I realized it wasn't an army – that it was an earthquake, although I'd never experienced one. I went into my children's' rooms and we sat on the floor in the arch of the doorway. I calmed their fears by telling them it was an army exercise and it would soon be over. That's the sort of thing my mother did in Spain when the sniper planes were shooting into our windows – she made it a game – told us to crawl under the windows and not walk in front of them and it would be alright.

Our house shook, paintings fell from the walls, but nothing else was damaged. I learned the next day, though, that a whole apartment building had fallen into the Tagus River and that the ceiling of the operating room at the Lisbon hospital had fallen in. That was significant to me, as the reason my son wasn't in that operating room was because his tonsillectomy for that very day had been cancelled due to his bronchitis.

Communication was seriously impaired by the earthquake, so I was surprised when the doorbell rang the next morning and the ambassador's wife was there. She was a friend of mine and we had worked together on collecting books from Americans who moved away, asking them to leave their English books with us. So, we had had a nice friendship over that. The reason she came was a call from my mother in Virginia, desperate to know how I was. It's a phenomenon everywhere that when you're in the midst of the storm, you don't know what the news of the world is saying. She saw that I was fine and could let my mother know, which was a great relief to her. I have since learned that it had probably been a tsunami which caused the 1755 earthquake to be so destructive. The world was not aware of tsunamis in those ancient times, but we knew. We were right on the coast and it would have been a disaster if one had happened. I've also learned that many of the homes in Estoril, particularly, were built to resist earthquakes. That gave me comfort for the future.

Chapter 16
Return to Paris

After four years, which was longer than we'd lived anywhere at that point, Mobile sent us back to Paris and I managed to get a Visa for my housekeeper/cook, Esterre. She accompanied the family when we moved to Paris to a beautiful apartment on the Boulevard surrounding Parc Monceaux . It was near the rotunda, and the bilingual school I found for Ken was within the park within walking distance from our home. It was ideal in that it was French/English and he could walk to school as I watched from my balcony.

Ken made a very close friend in his new school in Parc Monceaux and I was soon invited to the friend's home for lunch. The mother was so excited to have an American friend that she tossed the salad and, in her haste, included the paper towel in it and we both laughed heartily over white wine and poached sole. Ken's school work was so interesting. He learned his basic French very quickly because all of his papers were written with French on the left side of the notebook and English on the right – so unlike the segregated school in Portugal. At eight years old, Ken was self-confident, happy, very (damned) good looking, loved to skateboard in Parc Monseau with his friend, and, thankfully, I had Esterre to help accompany him in the Park because I spent most of my time exploring, shopping and walking around Paris.

The French apartment was unfurnished and I had the opportunity to contract with an excellent interior decorator, Claude Chauchet. Claude's wife, Irina, had been my friend in Fredericksburg when we were girls. Her parents had been refugees from Russia and were good friends of my mother. Their fall from grace was evident in the simplicity of the house where they lived in the country, but here and there were exquisite examples of their past elegance – porcelain, carvings and gorgeous tapestries which they had been able to bring in their trunks when they escaped Russia. Irina's mother had a flower garden with only blue flowers and raised sheep to augment their income because her father was employed at the Library of Congress, which didn't offer a very high salary. They were so intelligent and well-educated, it was a delight to spend time with them and discuss their life. Irina adapted well to her life in France with her successful interior decorator husband, Claude Chauchet, and they had two sweet boys.

When Claude made suggestions for decorating my apartment, he arranged the little furniture I had so cleverly that I didn't have to buy any more. He placed one of our antique French desks in the large entry hall off of which all the rooms led – bedrooms and living room. The living room had three ceiling to floor French doors onto a narrow ballustraded balcony and the bedrooms also had French doors. The dining room and living room were divided by an arched window, but the huge wall mirrors reflected each other and you looked from one end of the living room through to the dining room and felt that the whole space was one. Claude Chauchet showed me how to place the little furniture we had so that it was enough. We did have to buy white drapes – a stunning, textured white cotton (which I never would have done) and I used those yards and yards of material for drapes in homes for many years after that. They were pulled back by elegant fat French Tassels. To make our dining table large enough for the room, he simply added leaves to my small table of ordinary wood and covered the table with a beautiful blue table cloth. Then, we bought French bronze sconces for each side of the mirror in the dining room. Claude placed our second French Louis XV desk in the living room so that I could sit at the desk and look out of the windows. I'm sure most people would have put it the other way.

    Esterre had her room on the top floor with other maids of the building. All of the maid's rooms had Cape Cod windows which broke into the roof line and afforded them a beautiful view of Paris. I know, for a fact, that Esterre was very happy up there because she invited her Portuguese boyfriend to come live with her. I almost brought her to America, except that I could not get her a Visa.

    Claire, at twelve, went to a Boarding School in England where she had begged to go because her best friend, Ellen, from Estoril was also going to that school. On holidays, she came home, and I often flew to England to see her. One of the times I did go to see her, I rented a car at the airport and took off on the wrong side of the road down the M-1 Highway. A policeman soon pulled me over and asked me in his glorious English accent, "Madame, what ARE you doing?" And with a sweet smile, I replied, "I'm going to see my daughter in boarding school." He gallantly said, "Well, dear lady, please follow me because you are driving on the wrong side of the road," and he put me straight. Driving on the left side of the road is not a skill like riding a bike that you never forget … it had only taken a few years for me to forget. After four years of driving on the right side of the road in Portugal and dodging the dangerous drivers daily, I was the only American among our friends who never had an accident there, but I was not immune to memory lapses.

Rainbow's End

When I went to visit Claire, I was delighted to find that she was allowed to have a pet rabbit and we went across the sports field to visit her rabbit. He had his hutch with some other pets down there in the field and she could go any time and visit him.

Claire had taken up the sport of long distance running. She was such a graceful runner, although her equilibrium wasn't made for other sports. She was a natural artist already – with many excellent art classes. As I recall, she told me about the art studio which was open at all times and students could go in and use it whenever they wanted to. Claire had been drawing since the age of two, in fact, at that nursery school on Long Island, the teacher one day called to my attention that Claire had drawn a figure of herself watching a nest of birds in their tree. The teacher told me that that was very unusual for a child that age to have that kind of self-image and be able to get it on paper. I do also remember that by two, she knew all her colors. I always had a low table and chair for her wherever she was – set up for her to ply her trade.

Jim was hard at work as usual at his office in Paris except that he spent over 50% of the time traveling to other locations around the world for Mobile Oil as he was so sought after as a systems manager. Because Jim was so often absent, I pretty much confined my sightseeing to Paris and continued my shopping and cooking, although Esterre was there for heavy work. One day in the local market, I was picking peaches for our dinner and was looking for some to eat a few days hence. Markets then were not a do it yourself affair, so I asked the vendor to choose me some for three days ahead. She said, "Madame, if you want peaches for three days ahead, come back in three days." They were a snobby bunch.

It was a delight shopping – cheeses were in their special place, and a choice of anything you could even imagine. I became absurdly fond of cheeses, especially the pyramid-shaped goat cheese covered with ashes. Breads of every kind, just warm from the oven, would go into my basket. The dinner menu was created as I shopped, depending on what looked good that day. I never took a list, nor did any other housewife as I remember. I was thankful to have Esterre since the house was so often empty of adults, and I also had my good friend, Irina Chauchet, who introduced me to her friends. Therefore, although we only stayed a year, I quickly got involved in a pleasant social life in Paris which centered around eating and wonderful conversations.

Because I had Esterre for household work and could depend on her to be there for Kenneth, whom she loved, I hounded the museums – the Louvre, the Petit Palais, the

Chapter 17: New York City Again

Musee d'Orsay, and also within walking distance of our apartment, the Calder Museum, which featured an extraordinary room with padded walls so that children could throw balls and hoops and explore the intricate movements of his unique mobiles. Calder was the first to develop that art and the largest Calder I've seen to date is the one that dominates the center hall in the east wing of the Smithsonian Museum in Washington D.C. (also called our national gallery).

One April, I went to get Claire for spring break and to celebrate her birthday in Paris. My mother had sent a box of cake mixes for Claire's 13th birthday (April 10), so I read the directions on the box, translating it to Esterre on how to make the cake. I had sent Esterre to school to learn how to read when we were in Portugal, giving her two hours off each afternoon, but of course she couldn't read English. Esterre took all four boxes and emptied them into a bowl together, and deciding that she'd do the recipe one better, added seven eggs and poured all of this into her cake pan and put it in the oven. It rose and rose and rose – far higher than the cake pan. She cooled it and decorated it with icing and we all gathered around to cut the cake. The knife went through to a hollow interior. We had a lot of fun with that. The crust was delicious.

Jim came home for this special occasion. One reason Jim was so positive about my bringing Esterre to Paris was because he knew what a difference it made to have someone there with us when he was away. We had another celebratory meal that week. I had taught Esterre how to make a French soufflé, as I had many other French dishes. She loved to learn. That evening, we had a cheese soufflé with the entrée and a chocolate soufflé for dessert. Her soufflé statement, I believe, was "Madame, I have learned it well!" She was a delightful, cheerful person to have in the household.

That week of vacation, Claire and Ken enjoyed the small skate park in Parc Monseau, skating daily with each other. I had decorated Claire's room in that Paris apartment even though she wasn't there – with the two beds I'd bought in Portugal – white wood headboards with lovely flowers painted on them. Claude had put elaborate fluffy white curtains on the window and we had brought Claire's Siamese cat with us, who spent most of her day curled up on Claire's bed. An unexpected problem with the cat was that she did not adjust to being a housecat. She howled often and paced to go outside. I would put her on a leash sometimes in the evening and take her to Park Monseau. Her howling was so frequent that the butcher across the street once asked me how my new baby was doing.

Pets are a problem when you move a lot and we had been forced to leave behind a darling little black poodle named Bobby in Estoril. Bobby had been given to Ken by his pediatrician, who had treated Ken for frequent asthma attacks. In Paris, I found a doctor to treat Ken who determined it was allergies and, for quite a long period, gave Ken allergy shots to desensitize him against smoke inhalation, the smell of cedar trees (something which explained his regular Christmas allergies) and house dust. So we removed all feathers or wool rugs from his room to improve his environment and it helped.

Trips to the doctor in Paris were a hair-raising adventure. It was a long way across the city and included going around the Arc de Triumphe and other busy, busy intersections, crossing the same and circling the Place Vendome and then having to return for the same trip. The traffic was so fast – the drivers had a rule of Priorite a Droit – meaning that anyone on the right has the right of way. So, never look to your left – just watch your right and grip your wheel firmly and take priority. That was so frightening for me to do that, but if I didn't I'd stop traffic. It was a white knuckle drive all the way, but Ken did improve, which was a tremendous relief for us.

We had one year in Paris. Mobile moved their central office to New York. I could not get a visa for Esterre and we were both very tearful. She stayed in Paris with her boyfriend and I helped her get employment with another American family.

Chapter 17
New York City Again

Choosing where to live in New York took us some hours of study before we left. This was our regular routine – we would get out a map – pinpoint the office, pinpoint the schools we would prefer and take a compass to make a circle, enveloping the practical commute route for Jim. Then we would find a place within that circle. That helped us and the real estate agent and this research found us renting an apartment high up above the Hudson River, looking straight across the river to the Palisades on the other side – that's how high we were. The area was called Riverdale. It was an elegant neighborhood on the river, but we could only afford an apartment, not a house. Ah, the realities of life in America! The apartment was within a few blocks of my cousin, Glynne Robinson Betts' beautiful estate. She had a private tennis court and I would join her there frequently. Her children were the same ages as my children. To immediately have friends was a huge asset for me.

Once, while playing tennis with Glynne in Riverdale, I saw a brilliant small green parrot fly over the court. It seemed so out of place that on returning home I called the Audubon Society to ask them if there was such a species in that area. They greatly impressed me by pinpointing the area where these birds were living and thriving in a particular courtyard in Riverdale, making their nests on the window air conditioners of the apartments in that area and had adapted to our climate that way after escaping from a broken crate at the airport eight years prior to that time. These parrots were very squawky and loud and not adaptable as caged birds in the house, but they were certainly beautiful.

Ken thrived in his new school. He was in the gifted classes and they seemed to meet his needs. He made a close friend very quickly. He took up playing tennis, not only with me but on the practice tennis court that belonged to our apartment, where you just have the solid wall to hit against. I've never seen another place with one of those. Claire, however, was a different story. Her new school seemed to be undermined by gangs. She was actually backed up against her locker and threatened with a knife for being different. At the time, she did not tell me about this. I learned about it years later. Her mood that year was rebellious, as we had taken her out of her English boarding school to make

Rainbow's End

yet another move and she was demonstrating her teenage independence and angst. I didn't know any way to fix it, as I was feeling pretty angry and rebellious about leaving Europe myself.

Jim and I had rented the apartment with three bedrooms, one for each child and one for us – but circumstances made it necessary to have his mother come and live with us. She had been living in Miami with her husband and he had died. She needed to live with her family. Jim was her only living child. She had lost two boys in childhood, and I felt it right that she live with us. That meant that Claire and Ken needed to share a room to accommodate Mother Adele and with no household help, I truly felt swamped and unaccustomed to managing everything by myself. My cousin was a tremendous help and I spent a lot of time with her, but my mother-in-law was, unfortunately, a hypochondriac.

To demonstrate the extent of her hypochondria, she even insisted that she, too, was allergic and needed shots and would come with us for Ken's appointments to his doctor. The doctor understood so well her character that he helped me by prescribing sugar pills – placebos just to keep her from feeling uncared for. She didn't mean to be, but she was always ill and complained loudly. She had suffered a very difficult life – as a child, her sister had been killed by a flying piece of roof when it fell into their backyard while they were playing - her father had died early and her widowed mother always lived with a relative to take care of her as she had no income. Adele had been required to be a "very good little girl," so that the relatives would not mind keeping the mother and child. She also married her fifty year old husband at the age of twenty, and she and her mother moved in with him. She was considered incapable of really taking care of the household. She was simply a decorative addition, and decorative she was. Adele was very pretty. Her duties were to help with church social activities and her mother did all of the other duties including raising Jim. Another tragedy in her life really brought her to her knees when her first child, Lowell, died at the age of fourteen of ruptured appendicitis that was misdiagnosed, and when she finally brought herself to be able to have another baby, it died at three months of an obstructed bowel, also misdiagnosed. Jim and I felt that by the time he was born, she really had no more hope left in her to be happy.

Jim and I soon realized this was not the way we wanted to live. We both wanted to get back to Europe. In God's incredible way, we received a phone call from the President of Campania Diamang d'Angola, asking Jim to please consider coming to live in Lisbon,

Chapter 18: Carcavelos, Portugal

Portugal and take over the systems management for the diamond mine in Angola, second only to the Debeers Diamond Mine in South Africa. Jim had been highly recommended by an executive at Mobile Oil with whom he'd worked in Portugal. Our family jumped at the thought of returning to Portugal and contemplating the fact that we would probably not ever have to move again. The children wanted to go back to their English school in Carcavelos and this time, we would find a home within walking distance of the school, and Jim's commute would be in the train that conveniently ran right along the coast. Adele came with us to Portugal.

Chapter 18
Carcavelos, Portugal

We did our usual planning by putting down the compass though this time we were familiar with the area, so living in the hotel didn't make me feel homeless. The fact that the hotel was like a small townhouse helped a lot. It had the living room fireplace and dining room on the first floor, and stairs up to the bedroom level. All of this, with doors to the central pool. This time, I was in no hurry to move.

The home we found was in Carcavelos, a block from the ocean, unfurnished, but without any of the architectural delights that I could enhance so I had to dig into my creative suitcase and figure out ways to make my nest special for me. The most exciting item was the wallpaper I found with Portuguese tiles on it and irregular edges which I carefully cut out to follow the leaf line they printed and proceeded to stagger the tiles up the central stairs to the balcony above, where the bedrooms were. It was so realistic that even a friend, after many visits, told me she thought they were real tile.

My sister, Jenny, happened to be visiting Lisbon the month that I moved in. She has extraordinary original ideas. Just the two of us moved huge furniture and she suggested that we put my very large Chinese Mandarin Scroll above the fireplace and have drapes ordered to match the burnt orange background of the scroll. After a day of her magic, the house looked spectacular. Claire's room had a balcony of its own and she and Jim built a ramp from the balcony to the wall outside so that her cat could freely come in and out. Now age fourteen, Claire decorated her room in deep red, wall and ceiling included, and with a friend, dipped feet into black paint and with props and chairs walked their way up the wall across the ceiling and down the other side, planting their black feet all

Chapter 18: *Carcavelos, Portugal*

along the way. She then painted a white egret about seven feet tall across her door, so that you couldn't tell where the door was. I took pictures of that room and pictures of the embroidery she was doing at that time and some years later, when she applied for an art school in England, those pictures were immediately accepted as proof that she was extraordinarily talented. They waived the entrance test.

Ken, at eleven, took to guitar playing that year, and drumming, and Jim bought him a wonderful set of drums, which we often quietly regretted doing. He was an enthusiastic musician and had a marvelous teacher at the English school, who was as thrilled with Ken as Ken was with him.

My dear friends, Penny and Dick Howsen, were helpful in getting mother Adele into a bridge club, her passion, and we were off to a flying start.

To make things extra wonderful, one of my friends from our last time in Portugal was leaving and adored her housekeeper. When she heard I was coming, she firmly advised the housekeeper to wait for me, as she was sure we would get along very well. She was so right. Crimelda became the glue that smoothed over every rough event in the family. Jim had to be in Angola a great deal, mother Adele was more difficult when he was away, and the children's activities were eclectic and time-consuming. Crimelda was a gift.

Then one more huge event was piled on our plate: I discovered I was pregnant. I was forty-five, had not been feeling well for some weeks and went to the doctor to see if I was beginning menopause. "No my dear lady," he said, "You are pregnant." That was an astonishing announcement. Jim and I both took a few days to stop rocking in surprise and then were thrilled, as were the children and Mother Adele. Our surprise was with good foundation in that I had taken precautions to not become pregnant in a new country by having an IUD inserted and Jim, in the last week, had had a vasectomy, and yet, there I was pregnant. It was obviously meant to be. I cannot imagine my life without every single one of my remarkable children. I say this not only because I am a proud mother, but because it is the absolute truth.

I appreciated Crimelda more and more as my pregnancy developed. I did not enjoy the discomforts of morning sickness, afternoon or evening sickness, the clumsiness and not being able to see my feet. The family was very supportive, but the pregnancy was long. Before my Lisa was born, Crimelda's first grandchild was born and sadly, was found to be Down Syndrome. The love and spirit that Crimelda and her family showed for that child would be anyone's example of true love – in both directions. When I came home with my perfect baby, Crimelda very often brought her granddaughter and took care of both children simultaneously. The two babies seemed to stimulate each other when they lay side by side on a pile of laundry, with the lovely fresh smell of ironing close by, and definitely enjoyed each other's presence – twins must have a marvelous time.

Now, we were expecting a new child in our new life. It was an exciting time and we began looking for property on which to build our permanent home. We found twelve acres of property south of Lisbon, near the town of Setubal. It was a thoroughly picturesque setting that even possessed an Anta, so it was obvious people had loved living there for many thousands of years. It was an ideal tract of land with about half an acre of olive trees, a rippling brook, and on the hill above us were about five wind mills. We spent many idyllic family days picnicking on our property, testing different locations to be sure we would place the home on a site well-protected from annual Mistral wind. We could let it blow over our heads as it turned the blades of the windmills, creating that beautiful grain for bread and adding a consistent rumble to the sound of the wind. If anyone's ever stood inside a windmill while it's working, they would never forget that sound. It is much like being under Niagra Falls. A short drive further south over a mountain dropping down into the sea was a bay of such unusual fauna that it was designated a national treasure. We kept a small boat at that time, docked in the bay, and there were plenty of fishermen who were willing to help us tend the boat, moor it, carry us back and forth to shore, etc.

One day, two things happened of note. We were returning from an exciting discovery of the remains of a sunken Roman town and we picked up about seven roof tiles which were lying beneath the surface of the water, placing them with great care into the little boat. When we motored back to our harbor, Jim picked up the tiles to transfer them to our car and dropped them. We were both so stunned that something thousands of years old could be broken by us. We kept all the pieces anyway and our gardener cemented them into steps to our patio in Carcavelos. As we were leaving, one of the fishermen said, "Wait, Madame, I have something for you." From the bottom of the bay, he brought up a concrete brick with holes in it which I could only assume must be antique, for why would he give me a concrete brick? Then, with excitement, he reached into a hole and pulled out an octopus and that's what he was giving me. We took it immediately to the restaurant on that shore and they cooked it for us with its black ink. It is a dish they highly value, more so than I did. It was the same dish that I had been taught to make in the French school in Marseilles.

Chapter 19: A Sad Homecoming

Lisa's birth was an astonishingly unusual event. It's extraordinary enough to think that Claire was born in England with the queen's doctor assisting, but in Portugal, Lisa was delivered by the paramour of the dictator's wife – the most handsome sought after bachelor doctor in Portugal, and a celebrity of sorts. The evening Lisa was born followed a simple office visit to the obstetrician when he announced to Jim and me that I was already three centimeters dilated and probably should stay at the hospital. When I delivered Lisa in three hours, the doctor took my hand and kissed it and said, "Madame, you were wonderful."

In Portugal, when you deliver a baby, you bring everything you need for the baby including diapers, wipes, clothes, sheets – they provide nothing. So, we had nothing with us and Jim missed being at the birth because he was on his way home – twenty-five miles away – to gather the layette. The birth was so quick and easy — with a spinal block, which I'd never had – so I could enjoy the whole experience. The humor of it all, in my eyes, was that since I was so comfortable during the labor, I could observe the environment which was seven of us ladies in one room, all in different stages of childbirth, all the handsome doctor's patients and all hooked up to heart-beat monitors which thumped loudly around the room so the doctor could keep track of every baby. I have always equated that sound to a car wash – I love to go through a carwash. Lisa was born November 26, 1973, eight pounds ten ounces – dry and wrinkly due to being late – but by the next day, had taken on the glorious hues of a newborn, pink, shiny perfection. I noticed I'd finally stopped my eight months of coughing, so I must be allergic to pregnancy. I don't think any family could have been happier to have this little baby so late in life. She was our darling and has remained so to this day.

Lisa's first five months were blissful. Even Mother Adele made less demands on me, but disaster was soon to strike. The evening of the unexpected "Carnation Revolution," April 25, 1974, with the ousting of long-time dictator, Salazar, was a nightmare. The name "Carnation Revolution" came from the fact that no shots were fired and when the people amassed in the streets to celebrate the end of the forty-five year dictatorship, carnation flowers were placed in the muzzles of rifles or on the uniforms of the army. Not only were all prisoners released into the streets on the statement that most of them were political prisoners anyway and should not have been there, my beautiful Claire had gone to a party and, for the first time, had forgotten to call home to tell me where she was and how I could reach her. She had a standing eleven o'clock curfew and eleven o'clock came

Rainbow's End

and went and she did not come home. We were struggling to keep up with the news, which was very difficult. The embassy did their best to keep all Americans informed but no one could tell Jim and me where our daughter was. She didn't come home until one o'clock in the morning. We had called every contact we could possibly think of and when, thankfully, she did walk in the door with apologies for forgetting to call us, I completely lost my cool, screaming at her that she had no right to forget! Jim calmed me down but he was as upset as I was, and when we told Claire what had happened that night, we all shared our anxiety for the future. Rightfully so, for within a few days, the new government had taken over all the companies in the country and one of them was the family-owned company that Jim was working for. The communists were having no American employees. There went the end of a dream.

We were instructed that we were to be out of the country in thirty days and we were not to take anything with us that we had bought in Portugal. They required so much proof of every household belonging and its origin that we simply left everything except our clothing, hoping to be able to send for "legitimate" items later. All of our belongings, in addition to our twelve acres, were being left behind. The company held the mortgage and we had nothing to say about it.

Mother Adele, of course, was with us as we went to the airport. I had her one arm, held baby Lisa in the other, and Jim walked with our two older children. Mother Adele and I had sewn all the jewelry we owned into our skirts (they had no airport scanners then). As I turned from the ticket counter to start walking towards the gate, I realized I had left Lisa's folding stroller behind. I hadn't had time to worry about it when Crimelda and her son pulled up to the front of the airport entrance and ran in with the stroller, which they had found hanging on the doorknob of our front door. It was her final act of rescue.

We cried and laughed when we saw their car, as piled on top were all the remains of a wonderful gazebo we had had built on our patio and we'd told them to please take it to their home. They loved it. They lived in a walled-in compound on a hill above CaisCais (cashcash) with other servants, each with their own small two rooms, and shared courtyard. The gazebo, therefore, served many families for pleasant shade. They lived so beautifully together in that compound, sharing duties and even dinners. This is how they did it. The first home would cook their meal on their hibachi, and when their meal was cooked they would pass it on with the coals still alight, conserving in this way, an incredible amount of energy. Crimelda was so loved by our family that Claire, several

Chapter 19: A Sad Homecoming

years later, went back to visit her in Portugal and stayed in that little two room house. It's to be noted that she went back to visit Crimelda – not particularly anyone else. We just loved that woman.

During that dramatic year in Portugal, I did two things of note which affected the rest of my life. I had a beautiful baby and I reawakened my spiritual awareness. This was triggered one day when I was standing in line at the post office and met another American who had come to live in Portugal and we began to discuss how she was going to continue her Christian ministry. She inquired about churches – where I went, etc., and I responded that I went very seldom, but a good person to talk to would be the minister of the English church that we seldom attended. This beginning conversation led to a friendship with this lady, which became practically an instruction book for bringing me back to my undeveloped curiosity about God. We spent many hours together and she told me to read the book, Many Minds, Many Masters, which fired my curiosity even hotter and from then on I wanted to know more and more, but did not share this with my family. The reason I did not was because Jim had never wanted to emphasize spiritual thought, although he was an adamant scholar. His upbringing had left him with the feeling that churches and all that went with them harbored too much hypocrisy, especially when his mother did not want him to know or be friends with anyone who was black. In his mind, he put a big X through the whole business of religion, so we talked very little about God in our marriage. He was certainly not an atheist, and returned to strong beliefs before his death, but it just wasn't a subject we talked about. Nevertheless, I continued my searching and began to discuss Christian Science with my mother and went on searching, pretty much keeping it within myself until after Jim died.

Chapter 19
A Sad Homecoming

Leaving Portugal as a refugee with my family in tow was just as painful as leaving Spain when I was seven years old or leaving Aix before Claire was born. Despite the trauma, our arrival at the airport in Washington D.C. was jubilant as my brother and his family and my mother were so thrilled to have us home. We were going to live with my mother at Fall Hill, as I had begged Jim to please not find any new place to live. I could not cope with the problems of that at the time, and was pretty sure that I would need help with Lisa and that I would have to work at something until he found a new job. This couldn't have pleased my mother more. The very thing my poor husband had hoped he would never have to do was depend on my mother. God has His unstoppable way of teaching us what we have to learn.

Fall Hill did make a marvelous home for us that year and I was hired to tutor the special children who were put in separate classes at that time in public school when they had learning disabilities. As a tutor, I was allowed to be employed even though I did not have all the proper American qualifications, but only letters of reference from the school in Holland that had been supporting me in my tutoring in Portugal. As soon as I went to work, Mother became Lisa's principal caretaker by choice, and it was in that year that Mother and Lisa developed their great love for one another. Mother was magic with children and would pull out all her ability to invent stories and play-act and turn the woods into a palace. We also built Lisa a playhouse in an ancient Catalpa tree that year. The remnants of that tree house are still there and kept by the new owners as a memory of past children who lived there.

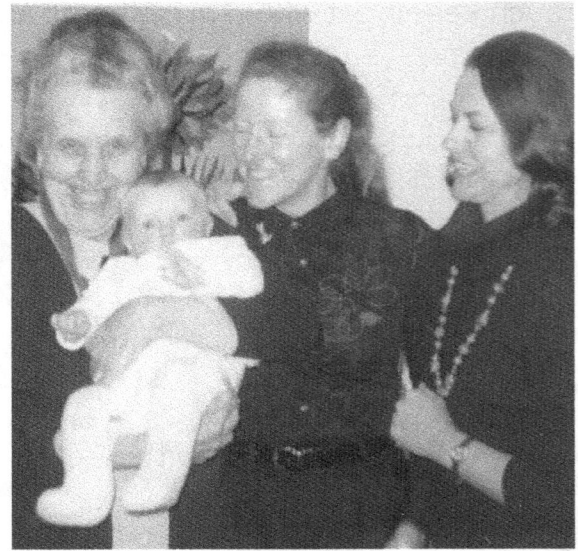

Mother Adele stayed with us at Fall Hill for about five months and I discovered the fabulous ability my own mother had to nurture and care for someone as frail emotionally and physically as Adele was. Mother helped me enormously with Adele and Jim was grateful. Five months later, Mother Adele chose to move to a very fine Presbyterian retirement home in Lakeland,

Chapter 19: A Sad Homecoming

Florida, and as a minister's wife, she filled her proper place and stayed there until she died.

Jim's unemployment went on month after month, much to our surprise. He was so qualified that he couldn't find a job since, in 1974, America was in a recession and companies were not hiring top management. It took a full year before Printing Industries of America in Northern Virginia hired Jim to re-write their systems manuals. They had all been atrociously translated from Japanese to English and Jim's skills were quickly discovered. He finished translating those huge manuals despite the fact that for many of those months, he was in bed, diagnosed with terminal esophageal cancer.

His disease was diagnosed two weeks after we moved out of Fall Hill and into our new home in Annandale, Virginia. Because of our decision to move to Portugal and cut our ties with Mobile Oil two years prior to that time, we had no American insurance of any kind and when Jim applied for a new policy, a physical was required before signing the final papers for acceptance. It was at this checkup that his disease was detected, to our complete surprise. We had attributed his extreme low energy to the trauma of being out of work and out of a home. The operation to explore the extent of his disease revealed that it had metastasized and gone far beyond any treatment that could help. I was in the surgery waiting room with a dear friend when the surgeon rushed in, anxious to get on to his next operation, and +-told me, "Well, Mrs. Macdonald, I couldn't help your husband at all. I'm so sorry. You will have to see an oncologist whose name I will give you through my nurse. There is nothing more this hospital can do." So I took Jim home.

Because of no insurance, the medical bills were heavy indeed, but his company continued to pay them, God bless them. Jim continued to work on translating the manuals up until the week of his death and managed to finish the books. During that time, I would drive back and forth to his office to deliver the finished work. I nursed Jim until he died on December 3, 1977, just a week after Lisa's fourth birthday.

The nursing lasted a long six months and his oncologist's empathy and kindness made up for the sharpness of the surgeon. I was even instructed on how to give morphine so that I could do it at home. A neighbor, the grandmother of Lisa's friend, began coming over almost daily to talk with Jim. Between the two of them, they developed great solace talking about God. The grandmother had lost her husband the year before with a similar illness and seemed to want to make up for what she had not done for her husband by doing it for Jim. That is often the way God works. The room was always peaceful after she left and Jim would sleep quietly for several hours. She introduced us to a minister who would come by periodically as well, and that's how God entered our home.

The two younger children came in and out regularly – Ken before and after school. Claire was away at school, but visited home occasionally. Lisa was often in the room with her dad, her cheerful little three year old heart bringing smiles and some comfort. There were four good friends living in New York that Jim wanted to see before he died and so I asked them down one weekend at a time. On the Friday night before Arlene and Bob Robison came, Jim died while I was sitting up in bed next to him, reading to him. I had only just realized that he was gone when, at that moment, his eyes opened up again and he said, "No, I want to see them, but where I went is the warmest, most beautiful place. The light simply embraces you and I'd like to go back, but I want to see Bob and Arlene first." He died on Monday. Lisa ran into the room and asked, "Mommy, what's the matter with Daddy?" I told her that her daddy had gone to a beautiful place and wouldn't be back.

Arlene Robison went with me to Lakeland, Florida, to tell Jim's frail mother that her only son had died. Arlene insisted, rightly, that we take Lisa with us. Ken, at age eighteen, could stay and continue his high school within walking distance of the new house and Claire was in the wonderful arts school in Brooklyn, New York, called Pratt Institute of Design. One thing I knew was that I was going to figure out how to make my life on my own and not fall into the easy solution of taking all my problems back to Fall Hill. My mother would have loved it.

Two years later, Arlene lay dying of the same kind of cancer that Jim had had and I went to be with her for a few days before she went on to that beautiful place. She and Bob had been dear friends all our married life.

Within two weeks of Jim's death, I took a job transporting children to the Diagnostic Center in Fairfax, Virginia, which tested children from two to five when they showed tendencies of having a learning disability. It was an all-day ordeal for the children with five

Chapter 20: Miracles Make Way for the Future

experts testing their cognitive, motor, learning abilities, early reading skills, etc. so that Fairfax county could prepare schools to handle their needs when the time came. My boss at that learning center said I was highly overqualified to just be transporting children, but I took the job anyway, as it was all I had legitimate qualifications to do.

Initially, I saw little reaction from Claire and Ken to their father's death. I showed little reaction as well. I held it all in, mimicking my mother. A big mistake, but I knew no other way. Subsequently, Claire began having problems with eating, sleeping and mood swings – so alone there in her school. Ken reacted by gathering a group of young friends, mostly in the neighborhood, who congregated in our basement which had doors to the outside. He had his drums and his friends had their instruments and they pretty much did what all kids shouldn't do – each of them hurting in his own way. We were a mess for quite some time.

I had developed so many respiratory problems, a new health issue for me, and my children, too, seemed to be ill constantly with one small thing after another. Claire had trouble with her skin and Ken's asthma seemed to intensify. Lisa, at her young age, seemed exempt from these emotional and physical responses to our grief, but the rest of us needed medical attention which I could not afford.

My dear friends, Jim and Adele Sebben [seven] (both psychologists whom I had met at work) recommended a doctor for our family who heard about our situation with no insurance and cared for us wonderfully pro bono. I called him Doctor Mac, and he was to remain an integral part of our lives for many years.

Miracles began to happen when, a few months after Jim passed away, his boss asked me to come in to see him and asked me how I was. I told him I was coping, but not very well. He then asked, "How much do you owe on medical expenses?" I told him the horrific amount and he handed me a check covering every penny.

A short while after that, the Social Security Office called me to come in and see them. Jim had thoughtfully left me a list of things I would have to do regarding Social Security and the Military and the funeral home, etc., but I had not yet done them all, and when I went to the Social Security Office, they sat me down to tell me that they had $800 a month for me and I believe it was $400 a month for each child until they were twenty-one, and I burst into tears and told them I couldn't possibly pay them that because I could barely pay the mortgage. The agent at the Social Security office jumped out of her chair, wrapped her arms around me, and said, "My dear, my dear – we're paying you – you're not to pay us!" Social Security also provided medical help for us until I could get on my feet.

Soon after Jim died, his mother passed away - I'm sure of heartbreak. To my complete surprise, Adele had set up a trust for the grandchildren and had put into it $75,000 – an enormous sum for a minister's wife with no other income. This covered their college fees to the penny. It was another miracle.

Ken, then a senior in high school, had been considering opening a pizza place in Texas with a friend of his when he graduated. Now, thankfully, he had another direction for his life, and with help from a Mr. Pope, who was an expert in directing students to the right college, Ken chose Marlboro College in Vermont, which promised to nurture his many talents. He did incredible pottery at Marlboro and then went on to the University of Michigan and graduated with a degree in computer science. Ken's talents were as diverse as his father's. At one time, he considered technical writing as a career and he was good at that, too. Today, he is a manager of a health food supermarket in Brooklyn and the dedicated father of two extraordinary children who he and his wife, Hillary, have adopted from South Korea. Once, Ken and I took a canoe trip for four days up the Rappahannock and at one of our evening fireside talks, I asked him what he would like to do more than anything if he could. He said that what he was doing was what he wanted to do more than anything. It doesn't get any better than that.

Because of her grandmother's miraculous gift, Claire could continue her artistic education at Pratt, and Lisa, at four years old, could invest her share to keep up with inflation and that share covered her college expenses when the time came.

Then, another great gift came our way. Adele and Jim Sebben had three children, all around Lisa's age, and because Adele's work day ended at three and I worked until six, she would take Lisa home with her and keep her until I picked her up after supper. It was a tremendous blessing. Lisa could stay with me at work all day and take part in the transporting of children and was actually an enormous asset. The children weren't nearly as afraid to get in my car to go to a strange place as they would have been had Lisa not been there. Lisa showed her talent for social work even then, and would eventually become a social worker. When Lisa was five, she went to preschool with the Sebben children.

Chapter 20
Miracles Make Way for the Future

For my future, I wanted a better job than transporting children. After a year of working, I envisioned a better life than returning to Fall Hill or just surviving on social security income. With that in mind, I opened my mailbox one day and there was an invitation to attend a seminar given by an A. G. Edwards stockbroker. His name was Fred Turk and his card announced that everyone should know more about their finances, so I went to the seminar – a weekly hour for five sessions.

As a result of the seminar, I realized immediately that I could improve my situation and should, indeed, become a client of A. G. Edwards, and present Fred Turk with the small amount of money Jim had left us in life insurance. Fred Turk had said at the seminar that no amount was too small to improve and those were the words that got me in. I became his client and told him my goals – to somehow have enough income every month to be able to quit my low-paying job and complete my degree in social work (which I lacked earning by one year) by taking courses at a nearby college. Fred took my stocks, converted them to other investments, and created enough income for me to do exactly that.

The Sebbens continued to take Lisa under their wing so I was free to enroll in George Mason University and began attending classes. On my second visit to my new stockbroker, he inquired how things were going and I told him that the hardest thing was the cold weather I was facing as I walked through the peripheral parking lot to class at 6:30 a.m. He surprised me by looking at his watch and then said, "If you can wait fifteen minutes, I'm going to take you shopping and we'll take care of that problem." We went right to Lord & Taylor in Falls Church, and he began searching through the coat racks. He seemed to know exactly what he wanted. He found it, but it wasn't in the coat rack. It was hanging near the dressing rooms by itself – a long down coat of a glorious dark copper color with a huge hood. He took it off the hook and asked the sales girl if he could buy that coat, which was

Rainbow's End

on sale. She answered sheepishly, "Of course, sir, you can. I had put it there for myself, but we are not allowed to buy the items before the customer has a chance to look at them." He decided I needed it more than she did and he bought it. I wore that coat for ten years every winter.

When he took me home, he asked me for a date and took me to a Hungarian Restaurant the following night. During our meal, I learned a great deal about him. His parents were naturalized Americans, having fled Hungary well before World War II. They left their first-born son behind with the grandparents and found employment on a dairy farm in upper New York State near the Erie Canal in a town called Scotia. After seven years of service, which paid for their passage, they bought their own small dairy farm and had six more children, Fred being the last one born in the early 20's. With great difficulty, Fred's parents saved enough money to send for their firstborn son, but the money was stolen in the mail and the child never came. Fred and his siblings always assumed that story was true, but many years later, after Fred and I were married, we learned the truth.

I encouraged him to take a trip to Hungary and find his relatives whom he had never seen. It was in about 1990 that we traveled to Budapest and looked up his nephew, went to the graveyard where his grandparents and brother were buried, and met two other surviving relatives and heard the true story. The money was not stolen. Fred's grandmother did not want to give up the child, understandably, and made the decision to buy land with the money, which lifted the whole family out of serfdom. They never told Fred's mother what they had really done. None of the Turks had ever gone back, so the secret was kept for decades. When we visited the gravesite, I saw that no relative had ever lived beyond forty-five years old. The evidence of the poverty they had endured was everywhere. One cousin who lived very isolated out in the country proudly showed us her sow, her tiny acreage of vineyard and her cow. She stroked her animals as I do my pet dog. She also told us about the horrific health problems of the family, and yet the smile on her face of pride for what she had compared to what she'd had at marriage was heartbreaking. As she passed around her large round loaf of bread which she held under her arm, slicing pieces off for each of us, she gestured broadly around the room with her right arm, holding the knife, pointing to the lovely stencils that she painted around her tiny two room cottage. They were truly beautiful. "You know," she said, "When the priest married us and I was sixteen, he said 'You will never have anything.' And now look at this!'" As I left, she gave me a piece of embroidery that she had done, and a painted

Chapter 20: Miracles Make Way for the Future

plate. The embroidery is exactly the same on the back as it is on the front and I treasure both of her gifts.

Before I left America, I had bought five lovely gold-wrapped stone necklaces as gifts for the ladies I would meet. I did not give them to anyone. They never could have worn them without risking theft. Fred sent them money instead.

Fred and his Hungarian nephew looked exactly alike. They could have been twins. Fred was 5'7" with a stocky build, thick neck, working hands, and when he wore work clothes, he immediately looked like a Hungarian peasant. He always dressed beautifully as a stock broker, wearing impeccably white shirts and good looking suits. His modesty, generosity and will to help those of us with small portfolios drew me to him. He was a wonderful listener and very funny, with  a risqué tinge of unacceptability to his humor which was often misunderstood. He had not finished high school, but had entered the Army at eighteen, thrilled to leave farming behind. As soon as he signed up, he finished his education with the help of the Army and got his degree through Maryland University.

Fred went to OCS and became a Major. He had an active military career during World War II, escaping death many times and even won the Croix [qua]de Guerre, the French Medal of Honor. He had a chest full of medals. The final years of his military career were spent in Intelligence, as the military educated him especially for Hungarian translation to help with the era when Hungarians were allowed to cross their border and escape German occupation. Fred was there when one Hungarian woman crossing the borderline, hands outstretched towards him, stepped on a mine in the no man's land between them and fell in his arms with her legs blown off. He dreamt about that forever.

When he retired from the military, he had a wife, Lila, and two children, son Gregg, and a daughter, Dana. He signed up with A. G. Edwards, a brokerage firm with a marvelous reputation, owned by the Edwards family itself. They trained him and he became very successful with the title of Vice-President. That's when I met him. never met Lila, because she had died of a massive heart attack the night Fred and I met at his seminar.

Soon after our first date, I brought Fred home to meet the children and discovered that he was delightful with Lisa. The older children were somewhat threatened by my dating, even though Jim had been gone for two years. There was also the issue of Fred's outstanding military championship as compared to their late father's more pacifist attitude. Jim had been seriously injured in World War II, after being drafted into the Army while in college. He had only served for six months before being shot by a sniper in France and had spent another six months in the hospital enduring extensive surgeries on a bullet wound that tore his back from the left shoulder to the right hip. Our children had been raised by a father who avoided even talking about the military and a grandfather who was a Quaker.

Fred was an elder at The First Christian Church of Falls Church, Virginia, a welcoming, friendly, church whose minister married us in 1980. Church had never been central in our Macdonald family life because Jim had observed hypocrisy during his father's career as a Presbyterian minister at a huge church in Brooklyn. Jim had been wounded physically and emotionally by the horrors he'd seen in war and spiritually by organized religion, so Fred, in just about every way, was his opposite.

About four months after we met, Fred's daughter, Dana, arrived from Lake Tahoe, Nevada, where she had divorced her husband of one year. She was desperate to be cared for. Fred encouraged her to go back to college and finish her bachelor of arts degree. In retrospect, I think she should have been encouraged to be an interior designer, as she was extremely gifted in that area, but college just left her with no incentive to succeed and she began using drugs and alcohol as an escape. After leaving college, she found a secretarial job and was soon put in charge of managing a department building with all the problems that the tenants brought to her for maintenance of their apartments. They found out very soon that she was also good at handling personal problems of tenants. With charming ways, she found new tenants for the empty apartments and soon had the building running smoothly, but her natural talents did not keep her from her addictions. She died of a heart attack way too young. I loved her and she loved me.

Our courtship lasted for one year, in which I began active participation in church and, because of Fred's help with my finances, I was back in school heading for a degree. During our courtship, I took Fred to Fall Hill often. He enjoyed talking with my mother,

Chapter 20: Miracles Make Way for the Future

fishing in the Rappahannock, walking in the woods where wildlife was abundant, and he generally fell in love with Fall Hill. In fact, he more than fell in love with it … he became inspired to fulfill a lifelong wish to build his own home, and by taking over the many repairs on the dilapidated condition of Fall Hill, he could fulfill that dream to his satisfaction. The truth is that I, too, had always longed to live in a Fall Hill that was in good repair and that was getting the kind of financial support and love that it required. Fred was not only a savior for me but for our family estate. Dad had been gone for thirty years and Mother had managed on her own, so our timing was perfect and was a wonderful solution for Lisa, who adored her grandmother.

Once again, I left college before completing my course and married Fred on May 10, 1980. And, once again, I returned to Fall Hill.

The first walk we took into the woods the day after we moved in was astounding. We arrived on the knoll overlooking the Rappahannock where seven oak trees majestically create a fairytale scene. Because we were standing still and simply observing, seven turkeys beneath the seven trees were unaware of our presence, and continued to peck for food and gobble until our exclamations of delight caused them all to fly into the air – circle the knoll – and glide down the hill to the river. Those seven oak trees stand guard over civil war trenches dug there during the Battle of Fredericksburg.

We had one party at Fall Hill soon after we arrived to celebrate our first anniversary, inviting our friends from Northern Virginia, mother's friends from Fredericksburg, and we "put on the dog" in that magical setting. We had Scottish games set up on one lawn, a volley ball net on another for the children and grownups, tents and a snow cone machine on another lawn and a bagpiper who strolled around during the party playing pipes the way Scottish ancestry would have played them. I mean, by that, by being up on a hill the shrill notes resounded in the air like birdsong and didn't burst your eardrums by being reflected by four walls. We had square dancing led by a wonderful friend of Fred's from his church, and my brother, Lynn, who had come down from Maine for the occasion, spent the whole night baking huge round loaves of his bread.

When Lynn arrived the day before the party, he asked me what the menu was. I told him it was roast beef, bean salad, fabulous mashed potatoes and bread. He asked, "How many loaves of bread?" I told him how ever many the bakery had advised for two hundred people and he said, "Nonsense. Cancel that order. You'll need much more than that when they taste my bread." I said, "Lynn, the party is tomorrow." "No problem, Sis,

I'll get started right now." Fred joined him in this escapade and they went to town to buy the flour and all the other ingredients necessary, came home, mixed and kneaded until the wee hours of the morning. Some of the loaves had to rise before being baked and thankfully, we had two kitchens to accommodate the baking. Our apartment upstairs had a full kitchen and mother's downstairs. By 2 p.m. the next day, beautiful, big brown loaves of bread were everywhere and there wasn't a crumb left over when the party ended.

Some months after the big first anniversary party, I found a lump in my right breast while I was in the shower. I reported it to Dr. Mac (who had once been our pro bono doctor after Jim died) and he recognized the seriousness of it, and that very day, had me see a specialist. After a needle biopsy was taken, I was scheduled for surgery four days later. Lumpectomies at that time were not considered as effective as radical mastectomies. I was very willing not to take any chances to have it recur and knew when I went into surgery that there was a possibility they would not remove the breast and I was thoroughly convinced that they would not, but they did. I stood in front of the mirror in the hospital and just wept in disbelief. One side had a breast and the other was covered with bandages. Fred and his children were there at the hospital when I was coming out of anesthesia and, thankfully, were there when I realized I'd had the full mastectomy. Their attitude had everything to do with my ability to completely recover and not to see myself as any less of a person.

The following year, I went to a doctor for persistent hoarseness and when he sent me to a specialist, it was discovered that I had a tumor on my vocal chords. They could determine ahead of surgery that it was malignant. Again, it was a miracle for my spirit to be told that this was not a metastasized cancer – this was a different and localized cancer, and would likely be cured as quickly as the breast cancer was. They were right. One great fear, though, before surgery was that they told me there was a risk of my losing my voice, as they could not determine how invasive the tumor was to my vocal chords. During the evening before the surgery, I was pretty mad at God at the thought that I may not be able to sing. It was, after all, one of my delights. Instead of sympathy from God, I got a reprimand. "What does it matter?" He told me. You don't use your voice the way I want you to." So, when I awoke with my voice intact but my thyroid gone, I knew I would be singing much more, as my God wanted me to. I quickly joined the choir at the Presbyterian Church in Fredericksburg, as the commute to attend Fred's old church where we were married, was nearly three hours. I just did it for the choir. I did not click

Chapter 20: Miracles Make Way for the Future

with that church as a spiritual home, and Fred did not attend, but my voice was being used to God's glory, just as He intended.

In the meantime, Fred was so profoundly moved by the history of Fall Hill that he jumped into maintaining that history, putting everything non-functioning back into good condition. For the next ten years, that was his priority. He replaced two hundred year old ceramic pipes, digging out their broken pieces from under the ground. He replaced the rotten beams on the side porch – saving it from collapse. He strengthened the major beam that held up the center stairway and even put the sheds into working order. He bought a scaffold and recaulked every window pane on the three floors of the house and even had custom-made storm windows for the basement, which had never had them. That, with the insulation of the ceiling down there, brought mother's heating bill down from about $500 a month to $100. We did all this together. He had to bolster the rock foundation on the old barn and he succeeded in doing this, even though he had to hire expert workers who all said it couldn't be done. The rock work that Fred did on the foundation of that barn is still a tourist attraction today, but the barn itself could not be saved. It was Fred's choice to make it his contribution to the family – now his.

Fred would go to his office three to four days a week and I was thankful for the rest. Even young people whom we hired to help us would say he could outwork them all. During those few days of respite from our Fall Hill construction work, I decided I needed to do some payback for the wonderful hospice care that we had received for Jim, so I joined the local hospice community and did the training necessary to minister to those in need of it. I found it very satisfying and as much a blessing for me as those to whom I ministered.

Being of a financial bent, Fred felt that Fall Hill had the potential to generate on ongoing revenue stream. On the sixty-four acres that mother had given me many years before, adjacent to the Fall Hill tract, we began a Christmas Tree farm. With this first attempt at being farmers, we experienced the disasters of farming. The drought the first year killed off the first three thousand trees. The excessive rain the next year killed most of the next crop of three thousand trees. But we persisted and put in a third crop which survived, and when they matured six years later, a policeman called us that one of our trees had been stolen. He had stopped two young men who had it in their pick up truck leaving the property.

Rainbow's End

"Please come and identify this tree, Mrs. Turk," asked the policeman. I answered, "Oh, let them have it. It's Christmas," but the policeman insisted that I do my duty as a citizen as they were doing theirs. After I found the stump and identified the tree, the policeman turned to one the young culprits and said, "Alright, young man, give Mrs. Turk the money she wants for that tree." So we charged him $40 and he left with a reprimand. We thanked the officer for doing his duty, but it was the only money we ever received from that tree farm.

It was in 1983 that my younger brother, Lynn, who had been born some four decades before in Marseilles, flew his plane into a mountain and died instantly in the inferno. He'd taken his small plane up on a day when he'd been alerted not to fly without instruments – but that did not deter Lynn. No danger ever did. He was on his way to interview an ex-head master of his from one of the schools he'd been expelled from. Lynn had been expelled from several schools, always because he did not like to follow the rules. When we were told of his disappearance, my older brother, Butler, who'd been in the Air Force, managed to have some Air Force Search planes look for him in the mountains of Vermont. It took three days to find him. My brother, my son and a close friend of Lynn's hiked up that mountain to search for his remains. My son adored Lynn and had spent many summers with him, wildly canoeing or sailing on the rivers of Maine and the Atlantic Ocean. Lynn had always ignored all signs of danger whether it was high seas or violent thunder storms. The adage, "There are old pilots and bold pilots, but no old and bold pilots," applies.

After Lynn died, I seemed to notice a similarity to Lynn in the way Ken walked and they did look somewhat alike. They certainly loved the same things and because of Lynn, Ken became an enthusiastic canoer and nature enthusiast – even considering writing in a scientific magazine at one point. Lynn is mentioned in several books on canoe making, well-read by enthusiasts, and when Jim died I wanted so much to do something to ease Ken's pain that I called Lynn and asked him to purchase, as cheaply as possible, a beautiful Maine Canoe for Ken. Soon after the call, Lynn arrived at our home in Annandale, Virginia where we had lived when Jim died, and his small Saab car was spanned by a 21-foot canvas/wood canoe. It was 2 a.m., typically unconventional, and in alarm, I said, "Lynn, I doubt that I can afford this." He said, "Bessie, over time you and Ken will have such pleasure with this canoe you will completely forget about what it cost." He was right. That canoe not only was a jewel of the river, drawing maybe two inches loaded, but I later had it converted to a rare canoe sailor by the inventor who lived in Richmond, Virginia. A canoe sailor is a regular wood canoe transformed by a sail that can be put up or taken down, and a rudder on the back, so that while sailing, you do not need to paddle. Years later, Ken took that canoe to Brooklyn, New York where he had moved with his new wife, Hillary Plattner, and joined a canoe club there at Brooklyn Harbor. His canoe was an object of photographic interest to all who saw it. When he adopted his two children, he gave up canoeing since it was not a sport they could safely engage in as a family, but I know one day he will canoe regularly again.

Lynn was a journalist and wrote many articles about unusual and reclusive people whom he befriended. Several were hermits on the tributaries of the Penobscot River where he would visit often enough to gain his subjects' trust. He would tape-record their voices. Lynn wrote a book on these people that he pulled out of anonymity. It was titled Profiles of Maine. He wrote another book, titled Respectfully Yours. He was written up in the Reader's Digest in 1985 under the title, "Unforgettable," by Mel Allen. This was a Reader's Digest series that ran for several years. That classic article follows:

He was everybody's naughty boy, everybody's Peter Pan.
That's why we loved him – he reminded us to be young…

Unforgettable Lynn Franklin
Condensed from YANKEE
MEL ALLEN

I first met Lynn Franklin in the fall of 1972, when I was teaching fourth grade in Gorham, Maine. In my class was Lynn's only child, a wide-eyed pixie like girl named Petra. Each day after noon recess, I would try to calm the class by reading aloud. On that day, as the children finally were settling, quiet as embers, a man burst in clutching a parakeet in one hand, a small cage in the other. He wore a leather coat, and baggy pants held up by suspenders. His eyes, deeply set in a lean, handsome face, glowed with excitement. It was Lynn.
"I've brought you a bird!" he cried. "You need life in here!" And then – whether on purpose or by accident – he set the bird free.
All I could do was stand by, spellbound. The children climbed over desk tops after the parakeet, which screeched as it flew about the room. Finally, in terror,

Rainbow's End

it dashed against the window where, mercifully unharmed, it was captured. Lynn had disappeared, taking with him my plans for the afternoon. As I read aloud for two hours, 30 children eyed the door hungrily, hoping he would return.

The next day Petra brought me a note: "I knew kids would love the bird. Am searching for snakes. And rabbits. Have many afternoons free! – Lynn."

I had never known anyone quite like him, and it was not long before we became friends. He was at once exhilarating and exhausting to be around. He seemed to possess no sense of time – or rather, his sense of time seemed unchanged since infancy. When his fevered energy was exhausted, he would nap, awaken refreshed, and not understand my reluctance to join him, whether it be ten at night or three in the morning.

He was a paradox: He'd lay his life down for friends, yet keep them waiting three hours for dinner; he was free-spirited, yet he began every day by writing a letter to his mother. He greeted friends with the cry, "Camaradas!" and a bear hug, then went for weeks at a time into the woods and nobody would know where he was.

"I LOVE ZEAL!" He was 36 when I met him, a free-lance photojournalist who found his stories in Maine, mostly among the fishermen along the coast and among the people in the north woods.

"Until you know a woodsman well," he'd say, "it's almost impossible to get a straight answer from him." So he returned again and again until he became like family to the hermit trappers, bush pilots, river guides, loggers and deep-sea fishermen. It was his gift to make them feel supremely important. In response, they told him richly layered tales that were published in the Maine Sunday Telegram under the title, "Profiles of Maine."

His impetuosity was legend. Driving with Lynn, I could never be certain when he might turn off and head elsewhere because he had "been on the road long enough." He drove an ancient, battered car he was always fixing, using parts from more battered cars littering his yard.

He was constantly just arriving or departing, and when asked about his trip, he'd invariably say, "There were a few incidents."

"Whenever we set off with Lynn," said a friend, "we never knew if we'd return.

Chapter 20: Miracles Make Way for the Future

But he made things sound so exciting, how could we refuse?" Said another friend, "He drove us beyond our capacity to be rational."

Typical was the time Lynn insisted that he and two friends could find their campsite 15 miles up the lake in the Allagash Wilderness, despite its being night, despite the wind, despite the swirling snow. Holding a flashlight over the bow of their canoe, he set off shouting, "We won't know if we don't go!" Somewhere en route they capsized. They pushed the canoe to shore, but were so cold they had to slither up the bank like seals. Said Lynn, "I'm the first to admit I'm often wrong. My zeal replaces judgment. But then, I love zeal!"

"SOMETHING WONDERFUL." A few years after we first met, Inspired by Lynn, I became a free-lance writer and moved to a cheap, rustic cottage on a lake. But still I resisted his entreaties to adventure, and I never joined him at sea, or in the woods, or in the air. And he never poked fun. But once, when he was learning to fly, he sent this note:

". . . And so cautious people wither and maybe never bloom – unless caution is a flower. What would it look like? Maybe a walnut is a caution flower."

Miraculously, Lynn was almost never harmed, as though fate regarded him as fondly as did his friends. When he was a toddler, he was always wandering off, so in desperation his mother tethered him to a harness attached to a clothesline where he could dash about without disappearing. By age six, Lynn had been rescued twice by his mother from drowning and once from the tracks of an approaching train by his sister, and had run away from home several times. "He was always looking for something wonderful that wasn't at home," his mother would later say.

At nine, he was sent away to school – the first in a succession, each charged with the task of "shaping up" the precocious lad. At the end of the trail, after his father died, after aptitude tests by the score, after a fair fortune spent, Lynn left academia degreeless for a shepherd's life in Ireland.

That was followed by an attempt to farm ("A mistake," his mother said, "but he made the neighbor children happy giving them rides on the tractor.") and a stint as a clam digger on Long Island Sound, where he lived on a sailboat sunk in a sand bar.

Rainbow's End

In 1962, he met a young art student, Patt Robbins. Lynn was 26, Patt 22. A year later, they married. They moved to New Orleans, where Petra was born, where Lynn worked the docks and eventually, after abandoning plans to salvage a sunken treasure, talked his way into a reporter's job with the Times Picayune. In the summer of 1970, the family moved to Maine, and soon Lynn began finding his stories and his adventures.

"THINK OF THAT!" In the spring of 1977, Lynn went to Greenville on the shores of Moosehead Lake, hired by the heirs to a timber fortune to catalogue and annotate their family and business papers. Despite the breakup of his marriage and his perpetual penury, it was a heady time for Lynn. A collection of his articles was published as a book and his stories and tapes of Maine people became part of the permanent collection of the Northeast Archives of Folklore and Oral History at the University of Maine.

"Just think of it," he said. "The archives could last a thousand years. The great-great-great grandchildren of the people I interviewed will be able to come and hear their ancestors. Think of that!"

Greenville is the bush pilot base for the Northeast, and whenever Lynn stepped outside he could see the seaplanes taking off and returning. He wrote his nephew Ken Macdonald, for whom Lynn had become a hero: "I've just got to fly with 'em, Kenny. I've got to understand what it is to fly with them."

The pilots let him climb aboard whenever there was room to spare. He went with them to drop sacks of groceries into snowdrifts for hermit trappers. He flew to Alaska, three days crammed behind the pilot, against the tail assembly and extra freight. He was publishing interviews with the pilots, but he wanted more than a story. So when a friend sent him money for a new typewriter, he rented one instead. With the money, he paid the bush pilots to teach him to fly.

Flying, Lyn found rapture: "I curved and dove and climbed and tilted the wings. I dove into craters and lifted on the upsurge, dove and looped, the sky upside down, like tossing Petra into the air and spinning her and catching her, holding her tight and tossing her again."

He sent me a card with one line written on it: "Here I am, where I ought to be."

"MY OWN VOICE." Lynn left Greenville in 1979 to begin writing his bush-pilot book, and he brought back to Gorham a pilot's license. He would buzz

Chapter 20: Miracles Make Way for the Future

his friends' houses and drop sacks of paper plates with messages written on them, thinking himself in a fine tradition.

He also brought back a personal myth that he, too, was one of the bush pilots, as though their experience, their sixth sense about weather, had been magically transmitted to him as he wrote their stories. He believed that, like a bush pilot, he could take a road map and go from Maine to Alaska without a hitch.

However, he frequently got lost. Sometimes he'd drop precariously low over highways, neck craned, peering through the window for road signs. Once, thankful that he had found an airport, he came in for a perfect landing – on the fairway of the North Sutton, N.H., golf club.

He was also trying to find his way as a writer, doing fewer of the oral histories that for nearly ten years had made his reputation. "I want to hear my own voice," he said. But it was a difficult transition and there were few successes.

Whenever things became too much for him, he'd set off on a wilderness trip in a canoe, taking only the barest of provisions, certain he could catch fish and forage in the forest. He slept beneath his overturned canoe like a Maine guide. It was then, in his journals, that he wrote in a voice as clear as a mountain river: *The way to cross a lake is at night when there is no wind. If the moon is full, the experience must resemble traveling through outer space. The canoe seems to fly over the water as if one stroke could propel it to the other side. The moon becomes six moons or twenty in the ripples off my paddle. Fog forms and drifts away and forms again. I can stand in the canoe and see over the fog, as if I am flying over the clouds. Then, suddenly, trees and rocks take on definition, and I am close to shore. The landing seems always a surprise, like the end of a dream.*

INTO THE MOUNTAIN. At 8:30 a.m. on Tuesday, June 28, 1983, Lynn drove to Stan Harmon's airport in Limington, Maine, to rent a Cessna Skyhawk. Harmon was always nervous when Lynn took one of his planes. Once, Lynn had rented a two-seater, promising to return by 4:30. At 4:30 Lynn had phoned. He was being detained at New York's La Guardia Airport. Unannounced, without permission, he had landed and scooted like a gnat past rows of jetliners before being accosted by the authorities.

Rainbow's End

Lynn had told Harmon this day that he was going to Connecticut to interview a former teacher he hadn't seen in 30 years. "I still love him," Lynn said. It was hazy in Maine, but the forecast along Lynn's route called for rain. Lynn was certified for visual flying only.

"Marginal weather," Lynn remarked happily before taking off.

Stopping for gas in Concord, he took off knowing he would break the bush pilot's first rule: Never chance flying blind in unfamiliar terrain. But he had always been forgiven for the chances he took. Not this time. At 10:01 a.m., Lynn Franklin flew into the side of Mount Monadnock. There was no charm to protect him from that.

A pilot on a sightseeing tour of the mountain spotted the wreckage. Searchers reached Lynn on Saturday, 400 feet below the 3165-foot summit, strapped into the plane that had broken in two and burned. Lynn had died on impact. It was how everyone expected Lynn to go, probably the way he would have chosen. It was just too soon. He was 46.

At his funeral we shared Lynn stories and laughed at his recklessness and his eccentricities, like his penchant for going into restaurants with a thermos and asking people for their leftover coffee. He had been everybody's naughty boy, everyone's Peter Pan. I think it was why we loved him so. It was a lot more fun growing older with Lynn around to remind us to be young.

I climbed the mountain with Lynn's nephew Ken. We stood quietly on the rocks looking down at the plane, crumpled among the trees. At 21, Ken was tall and wide-shouldered and already making his way as an adventurer and writer. He looked at the wreckage and then he laughed. You could hear Lynn in that laugh.

"He'd be so angry with himself," Ken said. "I can just hear him. He'd say, 'Next time, Franklin, next time we fly over the mountain!'"

My brother, Lynn Winterdale Franklin, Jr., was named after our father, and while his ability to earn a living was abysmal, his ability to live was extraordinary.

Lynn's ex-wife called us to tell us where a memorial would be held in his home town in Bangor, Maine and she hoped we would come. Fred immediately bought tickets for the whole family to fly up there, though my mother and my sister, Jenny, decided to stay behind. My sister felt that Mother was not up to it and stayed back to take care of her. The Memorial was exactly that – a memory – attended by both an ex-wife and a girlfriend, and two-hundred friends. The border of the meeting hall was decorated with buckets of wildflowers which his daughter, his girlfriend and I had collected. These are some of the memorable moments: a guitar duet written for Lyrr by two of his friends, which left us all crying; a young boy who got up to give a testimony to the inspiration Lynn was in his life – he said Lynn taught him to pitch a softball and when he told Lynn he'd gotten it to almost perfection, Lynn praised him highly and then said, "Alright, now do it from your knees." That young boy, with tears in his eyes, said, "I wish Lynn could see me now when I pitch on my knees." Patt, his ex-wife, and I hugged as we left the memorial. She had felt so separated from the family when Lynn and she divorced, and I felt that we healed our relationship there.

Patt was on the faculty of the University of Maine and because of her successful talent as a sculptress, headed the art department. His beautiful daughter, Petra, was named after the town on the Adriatic. Both of them had remained very much a part of his life. Petra was going to Bennington College in Vermont on a full scholarship and became a talented choreographer. The last I heard, she still has a business in Seattle, Washington, creating for dance groups. Her husband, equally creative in his way, finds discarded items of all sorts and thinks up ways to recycle them to be useful again. They live with their two exquisite daughters in an apartment that encompasses three floors on the top of the Smith Tower overlooking Seattle Harbor, with a circular stairway going around a humongous Chihuly Chandelier, a wedding gift to Petra and David from famous glass artist, Chihuly. Petra was a close friend of Chihuly for many years and he taught her a great deal about managing and building a business.

My only request for my mother had been to have some sort of legal document so that Fred and I could take care of her and live at Fall Hill for the rest of our lives. We did not ask to inherit – only to be sure that when we were old, we would not be homeless. Mother could not bring herself to write that document or any other document that would push her to decide what she might want to do with Fall Hill. She had a will – many of them – and would change her mind every six months or so as to the beneficiaries of her estate. This was difficult for my siblings and me and when I saw that no solution would be reached prior to her death, Fred and I decided to take my portion of land that mother had given me some twenty years before (including the tree farm), and give half of it to the City of Fredericksburg as a natural park for canoers and hikers to enjoy. The other half,

Rainbow's End

I deeded to my sister, which pleased Mother very much. My brother had his own tract given to him by Mother and Lynn's tract went to his daughter, Petra.

Petra sold her tract some years ago and it has become a center for canoeing called The Rappahannock Outdoor Center. Butler is holding on to his tract, and Jenny, too. On Mother's death, the final will read that the estate was to go to Butler (the old English tradition for the oldest son to inherit).

A December 12, 2003 article written in tribute to Mother by Barbara Westebbe in The Free-Lance Star follows:

> *Just as the loss of our trees depletes our oxygen, the passing of Butler Franklin forever changes Fredericksburg's mental horizons.*
>
> *She helped found an organization in the State Department that cared for ambassadors' widows. These wives gave up their lives in service, too, and were not cared for when their spouses died.*
>
> *She served on the board of the National Women's Party for equal citizenship for women. That would also save 35,000 or more men's lives a year because, if our laws were equal, our precious men would also be protected from industrial toxins. Old laws allowing a husband to beat his wife or child were being slowly changed.*
>
>
>
> *She helped individuals and kept hoping she could do something for education of the children of Bragg Hill, next door to Fall Hill.*
>
> *She met with the Rev. and Mrs. Joseph Henderson of the Tower of Deliverance Church on Princess Anne Street about our plan to set up a revolving scholarship fund at Germanna Community College. The teachers or nurses receiving the scholarship would repay it with 3 percent interest within five years of graduation to keep it growing hope for each succeeding student.*
>
> *She was our lighthouse on life's shore, showing us how to enjoy each decade of existence.*

Chapter 20: Miracles Make Way for the Future

When I gave the piece of Fall Hill that I inherited to the city as a park, it led to a tremendous rift in my relationship with the whole family, including cousins, who saw in this the beginning of the break-up of the old family history, which indeed it was. Within three years of Mother's death, Butler sold the estate and twenty-two acres to a fabulous family, the Kefauver's, who have brought it to an incredible level of luxury which no one in our family would have been able to do. I am thrilled with the outcome and am now dear friends with the owners, who include me in all activities touching upon any history being celebrated there.

I have since healed the rift with relatives caused by my deeding the land to the city. Jenny and I have found in our new knowledge of each other, that there is no friend like a sister who has lived your life with you and has many of the same memories. We've discovered so much about each other that we really like. Jenny married a few years after I married Jim. She and her husband, Francis Guth, also went to live in Europe. They, too, traveled constantly and extensively, buying exotic homes and decorating them and then selling them and going to another exotic home. Her husband was an international gourmet chef and she met him while visiting family friends in Mexico City. When they married, he had two daughters who became her beloved step-daughters. Much like my mother, Jenny married at Fall Hill and enjoyed a very happy marriage for nearly fifty years. Now a widow living in Orange, Texas, Jenny is a volunteer in an exclusive privately owned Bayou park where she drives a huge boat around for visitors. On her own time, she is taking breathtaking photographs of nature there – even to the extent of recently finishing a one-month course in advanced photography to enhance her skills. She is as enthusiastic about life as I am.

In March of 2012, Jenny called and asked me if I'd like to take a cruise for my birthday. I was thrilled at the thought and said, "But, Jenny, I only gave you a scarf for your birthday!" We cruised on a Holland America ship to the Caribbean, the Panama Canal and the Island of Curacao, the Dutch Island we had both so loved in our teens. Curacao looked sparkling, prosperous and bright, with its pastel houses of Dutch style, and our ship docked directly across from the old palace where we had lived and played with the Kasteel family. Today, it is an exclusive hotel. Sharing those memories and making new memories with my sister was a sweet experience.

Rainbow's End

My brother, Butler, has lived a quieter life and after his education at VMI, he entered the Air Force and married my very dear friend, Penelope Harbin, whose family had a summer home outside Fredericksburg. Butler and Penelope have one daughter and four grandsons. He is now in a retirement home in Bethesda, Maryland, where his family visits him often. My sister and I went to visit him last year and, in one day, healed all our old wounds.

Chapter 21
210 Brooke Drive

By 1990, Fred and I had decided it was time to buy our own home. We purchased a home at 210 Brooke Drive on the other side of town, also on the Rappahannock and also with civil war trenches on the property. Now, Mother could reign supreme in her safely refurbished home.

Our new home was a delight for me and the first home I'd ever bought with intentions to stay for the rest of my life. That was a heady experience. It was a one-story home in Spotsylvania County, which borders Fredericksburg. It was on a cul de sac in a small neighborhood called Country Club Estates. The front of our house looked onto the 13th Fairway of the country club golf course and out to the sunset. The back of the house was all sliding doors from bedroom to dining room and that faced the sunrise. Those were two of the requirements in our list of "musts" for a new home. I also wanted privacy in my backyard, which it had. We were one of thirteen homes in the neighborhood. The house was twenty-five years old, built by a lovely lady from Lichtenstein, Germany and it was in perfect condition when we bought it. She was a widow and was moving in with her daughter, having built the home to accommodate her late husband's wheelchair. She had

Rainbow's End

made sure it was all one floor, with three bedrooms, a den, living room, spacious dining room, wonderful kitchen, screened porch and a beautiful entrance hall. It was on high ground, two and a quarter acres with a slope down to the Rappahannock, where the Fred was delighted to find his trenches.

Even though we had left Fall Hill physically, Fred went over there at least once a week to do things. Sometimes, he even drove his tractor across town in order to work the old place. One time he discovered a buried hay rake on part of the Fall Hill property quite a ways from the house in the back fields. There had once been another barn and a tenant's house and a well that housed the manager when we were away. That barn had fallen and all its bricks were scattered in the ground. Fred salvaged those bricks for repairs on Fall Hill itself – a very wise decision – and while doing that, he found the old hay rake almost buried in the brush and he decided to save that, too. He hooked it up to his tractor, pulled it out of the ground and hauled it all the way to 210 Brooke Drive and we actually used it on our lawn at times when we had let the grass grow too tall.

Another time, he went over to Fall Hill with his tractor and decided to grade the driveway which was filled with potholes. It's a quarter of a mile long and not a small undertaking. Fred began plowing and scraping the surface and tapering it to ditches on either side. After one day of strenuous effort, it began to rain and it rained for almost twelve hours. Since he had rendered the driveway impossible to drive through, he could not let the job wait, but put on his rain gear and went to work to finish. At lunch time, I took him some sandwiches and with me came our new neighbor, John Blankenship, an engineer who understood the difficulties of the job. John looked at me in dismay as Fred continued to slosh through the mud and said, "My God, Bess, he's not going to be able to finish this." And I said, "John, Fred always finishes the job that he starts." By evening, the road was tapered and, due to urgent calls from Fred, the gravel company delivered new gravel to spread on the top.

At Brooke Drive, we now had a mortgage, but we also had the advantage of Gregg, Fred's adored older son. Gregg was destined to help us pay off that mortgage. Gregg had become a stockbroker trained by the same company Fred was in. After a few years, Gregg decided that he could serve his clients better by following Warren Buffett and he left A. G. Edwards to become a financial manager on his own. We quickly recognized his talents, as he took our portfolio and began increasing it far faster than his father had been able to do. Gregg and Fred also took up their passion for poker and formed

Chapter 21: 210 Brooke Drive

a poker group that met twice a week in Northern Virginia. One of our neighbors would see Fred coming home at 2 a.m. and asked him why. Fred explained that he had been attending his prayer group, and for years, our neighbor fell for that explanation. The group included a very wealthy widower named Wilbur whose eagerness and inability to play enriched all their pockets. A combination of Gregg's money management and the profits from those poker games paid off the mortgage of our house within three years. Finally, the widower's sons found out how much he was losing and put a stop to that.

In the meantime, I put Fred to work making wonderful new flower beds, as our prior owner had not spent any time in the garden. Fred dug up any rocks he found on the property and used them to border the flower beds. He was a master at rock work. In fact, Fred put skills he had learned as a child on the farm to make what he called a "rock boat." That boat was a sheet of metal roofing chained to and dragged behind his tractor. With a heavy crowbar, he would work a large rock out of the soil and roll it onto his rock boat and drag it to its designated location. He made almost one hundred feet of border around our flower beds. They were beautiful.

Until Ken took his canoe from his Uncle Lynn to Brooklyn, I stored it in my backyard at 210 Brooke Drive, covered with a tarp. One day back in the mid-nineties, Ken called and said, "Mom, how would you like to take a canoe trip on the Rappahannock with me?" I almost burst into tears with delight. It was a dream I had had many times. Ken arrived a few weeks later, his list for supplies and research on the river in hand. He said the trip would take four days and we began preparations. Fred and a neighbor helped load the canoe and supplies and drove us to the in-point near Warrenton, Virginia, almost fifty miles from Fredericksburg. Above the confluence of the Rappahannock and the Rapidan River, wide and turbulent, we launched with high hopes and waved goodbye to Fred and our neighbor Ken Glover. Within fifteen minutes, however, we turned the bend of the river to find it completely obstructed by a large tree. I was dismayed and said, "Oh Ken,

Rainbow's End

we've got to reload all this!" He said, "Not at all, Mom. You just take a comfortable seat on that sandbar and watch." He pulled out a portable saw and began cutting away at the tree. When he could move it, he made space for the canoe to glide through loaded. I was so proud of him, I could have burst.

The waters in a high percentage of the river were quite shallow and loaned themselves beautifully to poling. Ken was a master at poling, as the Penobscot River in Maine where he'd poled with Lynn was also quite shallow. All I had to do was paddle a little from the front of the boat while he stood up in the back like the gondolier in Venice and poled us through every light rapid and around huge rocks effortlessly, it seemed. The water was clear. You could often see the stones on the bottom, and the myriad of little mussels the size of a fingernail. The other delights were the frequent nests of geese and ducks and their babies hatching and following their parents. This was May – the best time to be on the river. We could observe the marvelous care the duck parents took of their brood and if any little yellow furry inch-long infant strayed from the pack, even a tiny bit, mother or father would quack with a definite scolding sound and that baby would rush back to the flock over and over again. Only once did we come across a stray and lost baby. We knew it would soon be eaten by a fox or raccoon or other predator.

When we came to the confluence of the Rapidan and the Rappahannock, I was apprehensive about our ability to maneuver through it. Ken had no such qualms. He told me to put the oar in the canoe and he would do the rest. I snuggled down with my camera in hand and took pictures of him as he expertly poled sideways, backwards and forwards until we shot out into quiet water with a loud hurrah! By then, Ken was ready for a rest and we pulled over to a campsite. They were simple affairs all along the river and always had a small supply of kindling wood ready for the next camper who came along. Ken made a bonfire and always cooked a good dinner – steaks and chops and all the rest. He had a big frying pan, followed carefully his list of what to eat first and what would keep, and we dined well every night. One evening, I said, "Oh, we're so tired, let's not make a fire." He said, "Mom, you have to have a fire." There was only one night with problems. I woke up coughing badly, struggling to breathe well. It surprised me because that was usually Ken's problem, not mine. He turned on his flashlight, got us out of the tent, and found that the air was saturated with flying bugs in a swarm, so he rekindled the fire, unfolded our portable chair and I recovered nicely, eating a delicious breakfast of eggs, toast, bacon and coffee with condensed milk. To this day, I don't use condensed milk without thinking of that trip.

At the end, as we approached our rendezvous point for the pickup, we found we were an hour early due to favorable winds. Ken groaned that we'd be sitting in a parking lot – a dismal thought after such an intensive connection to nature – so I asked him to pull up on the opposite shore where I saw a clearing and we would wait there. During that hour I did nothing but listen to the wind in the trees and learned that the wind has different voices depending on the trees they're blowing through. After a short stroll deeper into the property, I heard the wind change it's voice again as it blew across the cornfield. Little did I know at that time that that exquisite experience would help me immeasurably with the loss of eyesight which I am now experiencing. I can sit on my patio here in my home now and enjoy the familiar voices of the wind. I've learned a great deal about reflection and introspection, much of it thanks to my son, Ken, and my brother, Lynn.

During the many years since Lynn died, I have learned to be so much more non-judgmental. I mark it with Lynn's death because I regret so deeply that I surrounded my opinion of him with "shoulds," like he should earn more money, he should take better care of his family, he should avoid danger, rather than thoroughly enjoying every encounter with him and relishing his exuberance, his joyous outlook and his incredible creativity. I would have missed the whole canoe experience with my son if Lynn hadn't gone ahead with his plan to supply me with that beautiful canoe. That little boy who was born when I was seven and tried to run away even as a toddler, using my doll stroller to hold him up, supplied more joy in my life than I ever knew. He was so beautiful. His life continues to enhance mine today.

At Brooke Drive, I became an avid gardener, adding many more flower beds. Each time I did, I promised Fred it would be the last one, but it never was, and he never objected. We built a swimming pool so designed that it was more like a pond than a pool, and the plantings around it disguised it well. It was an enormous asset to the house. I also added a beautiful sunroom with a high ceiling between the pool and the house. When I first showed Fred my plans for the pool and sunroom, he balked and said, "Over my dead body," and I said, "So be it," and went ahead and hired a contractor named Ted Limbrick, who patiently saw me through all the changes I made as we went along. I was not a professional designer and could only go step by step. The result was

100% successful, though it took nearly two and a half years to complete. When it was finally completed, Fred loved it.

Back in 1988, a spiritual group began meeting at my home in Virginia. It began with five members. Debbie O'Kelly started the group using a church fellowship hall in town and our meetings were so interrupted by other church activities, including square dancing, that I offered my home as the place to meet. I could guarantee no interruptions. Fred would greet everyone with a big hug and then retire to the back of the house. He never attended our meetings. We met in order to discuss our beliefs in God and to share our questions and our faith. No subject was taboo. The group increased from five to twenty-five and we met every Tuesday night for nine years and only missed two weeks when I was out of town. It was my church, in a way, and even for some of the members, because I myself had not found a spiritual building that seemed to be able to nurture me, at least not in Fredericksburg.

One of my dearest friends, Joan Limbrick (whose husband had built our pool), inspired our meeting often with her spiritual observations and is one of the many reasons our group discovered Edgar Cayce's center in Virginia Beach. Joan is an accomplished professional artist and I have five of her acrylic paintings in my home in Florida. Joan gave our group a crystal bowl and taught us how to "play it." The bowl was about one foot across – an opaque white about a quarter of an inch thick. When you rubbed a damp shammy over the edge in a continuous moving circular motion, the bowl would start to hum a true note and on that note, we prayer folk would begin our meditation. I was practicing for myself one day, standing alone in my dining room, "humming the bowl," when I was so intrigued by the deepness of the pitch that I did not stop when my body and the table began to vibrate a little and suddenly the bowl burst and small pieces of crystal exploded into the room, covering almost twenty square feet. It was astonishing. I was not cut at all – it was, after all, a spiritual bowl. We never got another bowl. We replaced the bowl with brass Tibetan chimes, which I still use to this day for my own spiritual meditations.

After I put the pool in, I recognized a possibility of creating an underwater atmosphere for the dining room which opened to the pool area. When the meditation group arrived, I would turn the lights on in the pool and cover a dwarf mulberry tree with lights, put dimmers on the chandelier, and because I had a wall to wall mirror behind the sideboard, the water and the lights reflected on the ceiling and we could literally

Chapter 21: 210 Brooke Drive

immerse ourselves as we prayed. Our nine years together were not centered on studying the Bible. We practiced meditation extensively. We studied new age thoughts with enthusiasm, and read Edgar Cayce's books on his dream writings. As a group, we often went to Virginia Beach to Cayce's Association for Research and Enlightenment Health Center & Spa, where we attended many workshops, learned of his healing remedies, and learned more extensive ways to meditate. Twice, we visited an ashram in Virginia – an extraordinary experience of tranquility throughout the compound. I felt thankful to have experienced that visit as it gave me proof that there are pockets in the world where peace and tranquility can reign. If we can do it in a small group, we can do it in a big one. The example has been cast.

For Fred and me, 210 Brooke Drive provided a whole new experience of being involved in community. He taught me how to play golf and I taught him how to play tennis. We participated in country club parties, which included all our neighbors, of course, and enjoyed the shift from being so isolated by the work at Fall Hill, which had consumed us so completely the first ten years of our marriage. I plunged into the golf experience. While we were both in our golfing heyday, I became pretty competent and a dear friend from my spiritual group set up a golfing trip in Scotland for about fourteen players from all over the world. Joan's job was with the World Bank, setting up workshops for staff to learn to work more harmoniously and spiritually together, so she knew interesting people from all over the world and they were in the golf group.

Fred and I went on the golf trip. It began in Findhorn, the very north of Scotland, and our golfing experience would be down the coast playing on five different courses during the two week period. We were housed in a seaside chateau on the golf course. It had its own vegetable garden, supplying all the food. The first three days were an unusual preparation in the community of Findhorn with a meditation

Rainbow's End

every morning and the duties of the community were done by the residents which now included us. We all helped with housekeeping, cooking, gardening and serving delicious meals at the Chateau. Residents who didn't live in the chateau lived in their own single homes which they had constructed with old whiskey barrels, each at least twenty-five feet across and some made even into two stories. This circular way of living has never left my mind. It is a completely different feeling walking into a round house with no corners than it is into a square one.

One of the participants in the golf group was a Tibetan monk. He led our meditations every evening and included his observations of our deportment as it related to the golf game. He played in his yellow robe and sandals. He was a fair golfer and tremendously insightful. One day it rained all day and the course was closed. That did not deter our monk. He said, "We will walk two by two through the course as we would through life and accomplish our round mentally," and so we did. His greatest challenge was tempering one German gentleman with a Type A personality who could barely talk without wanting to tell his score, which was a taboo subject. Our golf experience was entitled "Fairway to Heaven." Score had nothing to do with it.

Here's an example of one our monk's observations: A player was faced with a ball lying in front of a tall pine tree and the green was on the other side of that pine tree. The player had to choose between hitting a magnificent nine iron shot over the tree and onto the green or taking an extra stroke to advance further down the fairway and then come back to the green with no obstacles in his way. If he did not make the stroke with the nine iron, he would probably have to take two strokes – one to get out of the woods and another to get onto the fairway. It was one extra stroke if he failed the difficult shot. The dilemma was, did he want to take that extra stroke? Did he have the skill to hit that difficult shot? And, just as in life, we make those choices all the time: Either play it safe or go for broke, and can you live with the consequences of your choice. Extenuating circumstances such as family and finances are often part of the life decisions. All of these issues we discussed in our meditations in the evenings.

Another golf trip arranged by Joan was in West Virginia in the Shenandoah Valley on a golf course said to be the oldest in America. It was privately owned and only nine holes, carved out of the hills the way early golf courses in Scotland used to be. The grass was cut by a flock of sheep. The golf clubs were all wood antique, no metal, and the clubhouse had a closet filled with clothes from the earlier era. The men chose their

Chapter 21: 210 Brooke Drive

two by fours and elegant spats and the women wore the long skirts and full blouses. Unfortunately, nobody took a camera. In the evenings, to our delight, we were to play another round. When I asked Joan how on earth we could play in the dark, she said, "You'll see." So out we went at nine o'clock and stood on the first green. It was dark and there were no lights on the golf course. The sheep had all gone to bed. We dipped our fingers into a bucket of wet sand and made our golf tee with it on which we sat our ball. Still wondering how on earth I was going to know where my ball went, I trusted Joan, hit the ball and it lit up like a lightning bug. And so it was for us all. In order to get your ball into the cup on the tee, Joan placed a rod into the hole that would also light up, and that's all we had to go on. Dark is not as dark as it seems – that was another symbol of life that we learned.

Joan once sent Fred and me an invitation to come to her dinner at her home in northern Virginia, and to bring no food with us. She called it a mystery dinner and we went with high expectations, as her originality had stunned us many times before. There were eight couples and we were told on entering that at the end of the evening we would be asked why we thought she'd had the dinner. With that in mind, we enjoyed three hours of unusual vegetarian food and, particularly, transfixing conversations. None of us had ever met each other before. Nobody came up with the right answer, and Joan announced, "You are all here because each of you have had a particularly fascinating conversation with me during this year." What a marvelous get-together.

Joan went to Tibet for a year and when she returned home, she was completely shorn – totally bald. This was no small feature for Joan, as her hair was her crowning glory – a shining brown, wild, unruly and curly – making a globe of bobbing curls around her head. She now transfixed us with these huge eyes – no longer overshadowed by hair.

Although we made many other meaningful trips with Joan, 210 Brooke Drive always beckoned us home. We had my oldest daughter, Claire's wedding around that pool and another wedding of my dear friends oldest daughter, Katherine Walsh, and also Lisa's wedding before we left the home. I swam every day, even extending the warmer months by wearing a wetsuit. My preference, though, was to skinny dip. Fred did not enjoy swimming at all, but did enjoy watching me swim from the bedroom.

With Fred's farm tractor that he had bought to handle Fall Hill's grounds, he now could mow our two and a half acres with ease. He also took on all the neighbor's problems when they needed help. He added a huge plow to his tractor and was the savior of

Rainbow's End

everyone after snow storms. Fred, in a huge warm jacket, was a picturesque addition to the neighborhood, driving his tractor up and down the street for days, either mowing grass or clearing snow.

One tractor incident that is not so pleasant to remember was when some years later, Fred was struggling to maintain his health and I found he had mowed the whole lawn without lowering the mower. His decline after a quintuple bypass was inevitable and painful to watch.

Fred and I had a conversation one day, many years before he died, in which I said if I died first, I would come back as some sort of bird to let him know everything was alright. And then I asked my unbelieving husband (at least as far as reincarnation) what he would come back as. He played along with me and said, "Watch for my tractor. It'll back out of the shed all by itself." His prediction, ironically, was carried out in a way after he died. As I sat on my patio in Florida one early morning, when the light is so beautiful, the largest blue heron I've ever seen suddenly appeared at my side, standing on the patio. I stopped breathing in astonishment, looked at the bird who I had not even heard approaching, and said, "Fred, is this your tractor?"

Chapter 23
Cameroon

One day in our kitchen at Brooke Drive a dear friend was visiting from Cameroon where she lived with her family due to her husband's work with the American Information Service (which is connected with the State Department here). She was in my kitchen because the State Department had asked her to accompany a young Peace Corps volunteer home because he needed medical attention and could not make the trip alone. Kathleen Walsh was highly qualified to accompany him as she is a registered nurse, a qualified therapist and a compassionate mother. The volunteer had been placed in the appropriate care facility and Kathleen was planning her trip back. She asked, "Bess, when are you going to come and visit?" Fred said, "Why not now? Let her go back with you." (Africa was not on Fred's list of "must see").

"Done!"

The rest of the week we used to prepare, with the hassle of getting the necessary shots and papers. If Kathleen had not known the right contacts at the Cameroon Embassy we never could have arranged my departure in a week (her own had taken three months!) Since there was not time for it to take effect, the necessary malaria preparation was waived, but only with written assurance that I would not be a burden to the Cameroon authorities if I got sick.

We were finally done and were as giddy as school girls going to their first prom.

The flight to Frankfurt was the predictable cramp-legged, chicken-coop long affair (an ocean is not interesting at night, nor are the movies for that matter, but they help). However, the flight from Frankfurt to Douala, Cameroon was marvelous. Crossing over Europe where I had lived so many years both as a child and a young wife with children, and then to see the Mediterranean and its coastline against Africa gave me goose bumps. The Sahara Desert took hours to fly over, its vast expanse of uninhabited sand making it clear why Africa had remained isolated for so long, developing its own cultures and languages. I could see cloudy pink dust thinning and thickening below and imagined the camel caravans and oases drawing Bedouins and other tribes to their waters.

The airport at Douala was steaming hot. Open construction allowed for the breezes to come through, but I would have welcomed air conditioning and quickly stripped several of my layers of clothing (already warned by Kathleen about what to expect).

I had time to twiddle my thumbs in the airport waiting for the interconnecting flight to Yaounde. Our luggage had been lost and Kathleen was literally in "hot" pursuit. While I was waiting, though, there was suddenly much action all around me – small rugs being unrolled on the waiting room floor and in the parking lot and on the sidewalk – the Muslims were at prayer. I was indeed a long way from home. Here I was alone, standing amongst these prostrate souls – and feeling very, very white; definitely a minority. That is not a bad thing to be every once in a while – a minority – it helps me to remember that feeling when I find others in that same position (travel is a great teacher). When prayers were over, Kathleen appeared as they were announcing our next flight. Most of the luggage had been located except for her bag with all her childrens' new clothes in it.

On our arrival in Yaounde we were met with the embassy car. I enjoyed my drive through the different sections of town … the definitely privileged parts, the market, the shanty's, etc. Privilege and poverty – this was Africa – but with this comes a lifestyle which entails caution, not the open freedom we have here.

We arrived at Kathleen's villa and a day guard opened the gate (replaced by a night guard after dark). I went in and was introduced to the staff. The cook, the maid, and the gardener were all pleased that I spoke French. A staff is necessary for the life there, as cooking is time-consuming without prepared foods. Boiling all the drinking water for the day takes time; washing clothes and hanging them up to dry, often scrubbing each garment by hand, for though you may have a machine, it is usually inclined to break down and need a part. Shopping is daily. Everything is fresh for the day, and storing and freezing is risky with the probability of your electricity going off. Cleaning the house is constant if you want to stay indoors without red dust, and you have to keep ahead of the

Chapter 22: *Cameroon*

bugs that look for the cool crevices. Mosquito nets are over every bed, as a precaution against ever-present malarial mosquitoes.

The weather was absolutely lovely if you went out during the cooler hours and stayed in your home or in the shade during the heat of the day. Plants were glorious, and little birds, unknown to me, darted in and out of all the lush bushes.

While Kathleen went about seeing that her home was in order I went to the garden. I was drawn immediately to where the gardener was tending a little grave and pulling a few stray weeds. I asked him whose grave it was. When he told me, it touched my heart and triggered my memory, for he said "This is the grave of a previous owner's cat that he loved, and when he left, I promised I would tend this little grave." Almost thirty years before, when I had lived in Pieve, Italy, my daughter's cat had been killed by the neighboring dog soon after we arrived and my Italian gardener had promised to tend the cat's grave for as long as he possibly could. I wanted to hug that African gardener for bringing back that memory and healing it in a way. To feel the continuity of my life across continents … that was one reason I had wanted to come to Africa. This was working out just as I'd hoped.

I stayed in the garden and enjoyed the light breeze. Over the wall I could see a formidable house standing alone on its hill. "What is that?" I asked the gardener. "Oh, that is the President's mansion and it is very well protected," he replied. "We had a coup a few years ago – unsuccessful I am glad to say - but it has made the president very nervous and he does not let anyone unauthorized come very near since then."

Speaking of security, however, it is so much more in the American awareness than it was even four years ago (1990 was the year). The area where Americans live is on one side of town, the embassy in the middle and the school opposite. It is of great concern to parents that they would be so separated from their children and vice versa – in case of more trouble. Our government is trying to do its best toward that threat all over the world, and it is a big expensive problem.

We were finally ready to go to the children's school, for we were very anxious to reunite with the girls.

A joyous reunion it was! But we found the youngest little girl, Fran, had a heavy bandage on her sandaled foot. "What is THIS?" asked her nurse/mother. "Well," said Fran, "a little cut I had just quickly got terribly infected. It is really better now." Scowls

Rainbow's End

from her mother, feeling her little one had been neglected … it is pretty hard to replace Kathleen's vigilance. She, who never went far in that country without disinfectants of some kind.

There was a worse piece of sobering news that one of the teachers had gone to the coast for a weekend and contracted some terrible disease and died within three days – the school was in deep mourning over the death.

As we were hearing all this, Fran's teacher came up to Kathleen and asked if she could possibly take time to go to see her father for a visit. He was a missionary/doctor in a town called Matete, about half a day away by car, and needed Kathleen to help him with a few operations for which he had no other assistance at that time.

The next day we prepared to go to Matete.

We packed the car with fresh bread as a gift, and with some other things we would need, and set out after the children left for school, only to be stopped before leaving the outskirts of town by a policeman, saying no, indeed, that we could not go further. The roads were closed because the president was going to see his mother (near Matete) and while he was traveling, no other cars were to be on the road. So we waited.

Finally, we were given the go ahead and sped off; the upside to this being that the roads had been watered to keep down the dust and we profited from it. The memory of the coup was still fresh and probably always would be. A sobering thought.

We arrived at Matete at lunch time while the school bell was ringing for recess. The mission was a school, a hospital and a spiritual haven all in one. We entered the lovely and very old residence of the Freeman's (the missionaries). It was a gracious, cool home with natural wood around the doors and windows, the stairs and the porch framing. The stone floors with grass mats complemented the wood. Children's pictures and other simple family mementos were placed here and there. It was simple and homey – cared for with love.

A large generator grumbled nearby. "It needs some work," said Dr. Freeman as he came in, "and I will get to it as soon as I can. We can't do without that!"

Our bread was a hit, for the Freemans had little time for kneading and raising dough and they and Kathleen caught up with the news from town.

As we were drinking our delicious Cameroonian coffee (one of the products Cameroon exported), a helper came in to show Dr. Freeman a tool he had made for a particular surgical procedure. "I need this for a hernia," said Dr. Freeman. "My old one broke."

Chapter 22: Cameroon

"Was it hard to file into shape?" asked Dr. Freeman.

"Oh yes sir, it took me a long time. The metal was very hard."

"I should have told you. I'm sorry. Next time you will find it easier if you heat the metal as you go. I'm sorry I didn't tell you that."

This little incident demonstrated the patience required to live there. You needed to be constantly teaching, as the following interruption also demonstrated.

A fight in the school yard required Mrs. Freeman to intervene and when she returned she was saddened to have found that the argument had been over a ball point pen. "Just a ball point pen," she said. "It means so much to them."

Dr. Freeman rose from the table. "I have to get to the hospital," he said. "Kathleen if you would come in about an hour I think I will be ready to start." He explained that it takes that much time to just go over the x-rays with the families. If they feel they understand they will be calm, and then the patient will be calm and heal faster. It is worth the trouble. "Bess," he said, "you may want to come over and see what the hospital is like and then I am sure Mrs. Freeman would appreciate your help in the schoolroom for a few hours. The children love to have someone new to show off to." I thought to myself that this was a lovely positive way to present learning – I was not going to help them learn, I was to be the recipient of their pride in learning!

Have we got something backwards in America?

The hospital was laid out with rows of rooms each opening to an arcade. On this arcade, the families who had brought their ailing member set up camp, made a small fire and put down their rugs to sleep on. They were the "nurses," and would feed and bathe their patient. They shared food when available (although I did not think the drying porcupine so appetizing as they did!) and they had good well water with which to wash their grinding stones and utensils.

Smaller children played nearby, quietly, using whatever they fashioned from nature as toys. There was great reverence for the care they were being given, and some families had walked for days to bring their loved one here.

After the surgeries, we decided to go back to Yaounde and not stay the night since Kathleen was missing her daughters and felt she had left them long enough. We could also benefit from the watered down road and the cooler night air, which made things more pleasant. On the trip home, Kathleen told me how the Freeman's financed their operation. There was often not enough from the church to pay for all they did so they would return to California, their home, and Dr. Freeman would take up his practice until he had saved enough money to replenish supplies he needed in the hospital. Then they would return to Matete to continue their service.

What an extraordinary couple! Their daughter (the teacher I'd met at Fran's school) married a young American I had met while there and I was privileged to be asked to their wedding.

Back in Yaounde next day we went to a party at the Ambassador's home. It was a good opportunity for me to meet the other foreign service employees and the other embassy personnel. Cameroon is a sought after African nation. It is stable and has many resources and is blessed with a good government. The Ambassador invited me to take the place of an ailing consular employee who was to have gone on a long-planned trip to Engoundere in the north, near Chad, and visit the village of a prosperous tribe. It was an unusual invitation, he said, and he thought I would really enjoy it. It would be an opportunity to see the "inside" of an African village. I jumped at the chance and extended my stay accordingly.

Next day we began to prepare for our trip north. Kathleen and I went to market to be sure the cook had what he needed to take care of Mr. Walsh during our absence. It had been Neil Walsh who backed up the Ambassador and funded my trip, so we wanted to make sure he was well taken care of. Kathleen and Neil Walsh were extraordinary in both the foreign service and as parents. The girls would need a few items of new clothing, too, and it was a good opportunity for me to see what shopping was like.

"Comfortable flat shoes, first thing," advised Kathleen, "and be sure and bring the bags and baskets to hold the groceries. Nobody is going to wrap up your food in paper bags!"

The market was bustling … food in one section, clothing in another, meats lined up in the open air, chicken and other poultry separately, and then home-cooked items apart from that. It was going to be a busy "walking" day to get everything we needed. Around the periphery on the streets were real shops such as bakeries and candy stores, and these stayed open even after the outdoor market closed at about three in the afternoon. About that time activity picked up a bit as bargains were to be had to save the merchants from having to take everything home again. Some items were controlled by law to not be kept over another day. It surprised me that there was some control on items which might go bad after sitting in the heat.

Chapter 22: Cameroon

A sight which was not comfortable to see was Africans stricken with leprosy. It is a sobering sight to see such a disease and to be so near the sufferers of it. A more cheerful sight was three women in their brilliant caftans squatting before gourds used as bowls and filled with home grown produce. One merchant particularly attracted me for she had five or six circular bowls filled with circular vegetables and they created something so beautiful that I asked if I could take her picture. She said, "If you give me $50!" DOLLARS! She laughed and I laughed but she did not want me to take her picture so we moved on to the clothing section where I found caftans. The merchant had thoughtfully provided a standing mirror right there for the purchaser to admire himself and for others to watch you while they nodded approval or disapproval. It was a very friendly event, and then, of course, the bargaining. I bought three which were approved of and Kathleen's girls found the shirts they needed but they were not about to try them on there. I was not done, though, for I was also out to find something which I hoped would be unusual for Lisa's middle school graduation.

Way back in the labyrinth of stalls were other clothes of all sorts with *men* sitting at sewing machines putting the embroidery on the robes. I did find a dress hanging high on a pole. It was white with lovely cut embroidery and fine lace on the sleeves – perfect – how much? $40 said the African. I asked if he had made it and he said, "No, this dress was brought from France!" I was surprised and wondered how many other countries traded. Around me were also tables and tables of folded yard goods, precut with pieces just right for making a caftan with a turban to match. The choice was abundant, the styles and colors were of myriad number and some of the designs were "this year," (said the merchant) and some of last year, etc.

For example, when the Pope was expected for a visit, special yard goods were printed with his portrait on them – big heads – repeated all over! And the extra yardage for the head covering – I am sure you can imagine the spectacle of the people waving and jubilant and smothered with pope images – men, women and children!

That afternoon we accepted another invitation, this time from Mr. Noah, grandfather to the famous tennis player, "NOAH." At that time I was very "into" tennis and grandson Noah, as the world knew him, was one of the top ten players in the world and this was his hometown. The grandfather loved to be with Americans. He told us his wife was American-born and he would like us to meet her. He also wanted us to bring one of the white kittens from the litter of kittens Kathleen's cat had had. His wife had heard about it and asked Mr. Noah to please ask Kathleen to bring her a kitten.

So, we went "to tea." I was thrilled to have the opportunity to see another side of how a Youandian lived. The villa was modest but filled with domestic help. The shutters were all closed against dust and sun and we entered the cleanest house you can imagine. The floors were white marble, the furniture cream leather and glass built-in shelves (very modern) lined the walls to display a fabulous collection of African art (of which I am very fond). One huge (about seven feet high) carved elephant head of black teak was studded with white shells and copper coins in concentrated design. "The more shells, the richer the work," I was told. Porcelain and ceramic, too, were displayed, along with large and small drums and smaller pieces of beautifully carved images that delighted the eye. There were bronze bells and an assortment of beads as well.

We were introduced to Mr. Noah's wife and were stunned to see she was probably only in her twenties. She had been a successful model in America and moved with marked grace and beauty. A nurse soon brought in their two year old son, a very active child. I could see the parents were in worship-mode and also in shock. He proceeded to pick up the beautiful things with no mind to caring for them. It was quickly obvious that he was seldom in this room, and certainly never alone, for within minutes, several items were being hurled through the opening in the shutters. He was quickly removed to his playroom.

While Kathleen and I were balancing lovely cups of tea, we were giving one another uncomfortable glances as we considered the fate of the little white kitten who at that moment was still curled up in the basket under my chair. The beautiful young Mrs. Noah caught our exchange and reassured us, somewhat, that this kitten was for her and would live in her rooms, not those of her son. Well, we were rather caught now, and ultimately, seeing how the little boy did seem to have his restricted space clearly defined, we did leave the kitten.

On we went to another social occasion … a birthday party in another villa with adults, children, all their friends, all their relatives and close family, the childrens' teachers and playmates – all were invited. The room was cleared in the center with all the furniture unceremoniously against the walls. A table was covered with bottled soft drinks of every kind, harder liquor on another table, and friends fiddling and drumming with vigor. It was

Chapter 22: *Cameroon*

marvelously festive and welcoming, all ages dancing together from wobbly grandfather to toddling baby. What a celebration of generations!

As we danced out to our car, we capped off our social whirl by one more visit to the studio and home of an artist friend of Kathleen's – an American whose husband was connected with the embassy. Here was yet another way to live. An elegant villa was revealed as we drove through the high stone walls. The artist herself had renovated it. Brilliant flowers tumbling over the walls, even a lawn and flower beds of exotic plants, spacious rooms and efficient, courteous household staff maintaining the comfort and elegance of it all. The stunning paintings were modern and crisp and the night sounds of traffic and voices of domestic living could be softly heard from outside the wall. It was quite a haven, and we ended our day with hugs and promises to return before I left Cameroon. The next day was packing day and then off to the airport for our trip to Engoundere. We were all pretty excited, the children especially, but I was apprehensive when I noted the very careful weighing of ALL our luggage, including our hand luggage and the rather (what looked to me like rusty appearance of the airplane). I mentioned this to Kathleen and she laughingly said, "Oh Bess, you should have seen the one they *used* to have!"

I was used to observing small planes with a critical eye for Jim had been quality control engineer (early in his career with Republic), and repairs for the planes NATO bought were his responsibility.

We took off and landed without incident, but the expanse of uninterrupted jungle below us quite sobered me. However, on landing, we were met by a "fleet" of three Volkswagen buses of aged vintage, painted wildly to look like yellow zebra's. They were not air conditioned but did have screens on the windows, which did not seem to help much in keeping out the pinkish dust (much like the dust from Virginia brick, interestingly enough). Our baggage was stored in open racks on top of the buses and fresh water was evidently supplied in copious amounts.

Off we went, three buses full, the drivers handsome and stylishly robed with bright circular embroidered caps.

Our first stop was at a remarkable lake which had been formed by a volcano. The fact that there was a lake at all was what made the stop of interest; sandwiches were supplied and we ate while sitting on a platform of a lookout house built for the purpose. The silence was wonderful, some birds could be heard, and the dryness of the trees was evident – you could feel the Sahara very near.

Rainbow's End

I walked over to a particular tree which seemed to have flowers on it, but found they were thick nuts similar to the Chinese chestnut in the way it opened without the spines, their thickness demonstrated the need for protection of the fruit from these dry conditions and from animals that would eat them all keeping them from ever propagating when they fell to the ground. It reminded me of Lynn's quote – "Perhaps the walnut is a caution flower." We absorbed the silence in appreciation and then piled into our three little buses and went on to our destination for the night. The Ambassador was invited to sit in the first bus and thereby have less dust, however, our own bus was so lively with the children and some of the Embassy staff (practically comedians) that I saw the Ambassador and his group looking rather longingly at our bus after we had stopped for another little stretch break.

We arrived by evening at a marvelous Quinta (farm) owned by a Frenchman. His family had bought it when Cameroon was under the French and it had been used for purely personal and private hunting parties. The present government, I was told, did not allow the land to be sold or used for such private enterprises anymore.

The Quinta supplied us comfortably with all our needs. The guest houses were round, built of stone with thatched roofs. They slept about four to each house. We had a sink but the showers and toilets were down a path in the center of the houses much as the arrangement sometimes is for campers in America. The Quinta had a much loved lake with a little row boat for our use which we and the children quickly took advantage of. We would have loved to swim, but were told the water was not safe for that. The Quinta had its own vegetable and flower garden. The main house had a huge outdoor terrace, in fact, it was mostly terrace with low paladian style walls with open arches supporting a magnificent thatched roof. All our meals were taken on that fine terrace.

The kitchen, which I stumbled upon when lost (and I don't think they wanted us to see it) was rather an outdoor pit with ovens on either side. All the delicious food seemed to come from there. I saw no indoor kitchen – only a row of little rooms with doors probably for supplies.

In the arcs of brick around the dining room there were beautiful bronze statues of horses which I fell in love with and vowed I would try to find one to buy and take home. I also loved the huge (even five foot long) drums which hung on the walls. One was used to summon us to meals and the others were played by the staff when they were off duty. It was a thrilling sound, especially in the evening as we watched a rim of fire in the

Chapter 22: Cameroon

distance all around the Quinta – the owner explained that burning was the accepted way of ridding the land of grass to prepare the field for other crops.

Our first dinner was shish-ka-bobs of firm fish, skewered with peppers, onions and tomatoes – all from the gardens, of course. Before dessert, we were honored to have the head of the fish we ate displayed for us, a monstrous creature with a neck almost nine inches high! And they said it was caught in their lake!

With the treat of strawberry short cake and the strawberries with the flavor of our wild strawberries at home, we felt truly replete and shuffled off to our respective huts for the night. I slept in one with two of the girls and Kathleen in another with the younger child. We all felt we were in camp! We kept a flashlight ready for the night trip to the "facilities." No untoward events or African wildlife interrupted our sleep.

Breakfast was as delicious as the dinner. Before breakfast we had gone to the lake and witnessed an incredible sight of thousands of egrets flying out of their roost in a tree by the side of the lake. We took the little row boat out to be near them, and truly, there were so many of them that the tree looked white as a Christmas tree might after you have covered it with every ornament you had collected and then added spray snow. There is a picture that shows the tree after we had scared most of the birds away.

While we were breakfasting, our buses were being loaded with the days supply for a picnic lunch and, of course, stashed with the ever-present bottles of water.

Stopping for lunch was something to look forward to. We had begun to learn that you never knew where you would be for that repast. Sometimes it had to be on the side of the road with no substantial shade while you were waiting for one of the buses to be repaired. This happened at least twelve times during the week! After all, one bus would have the spare tire but another would have the wrench. Therefore, one driver had to notice that the other was not there and then turn back to help out. The official "road flare" was obtained by going into the bush along the side of the road and finding as big a branch as you could find and then running back some few hundred yards and placing the branch in the middle of the road – you needed to put the flare well back of the bus, especially if you were around a corner. African drivers seemed to push their vehicle as fast as they would go even though proof of the danger of doing this was evident along the side of the road where the rusting carcasses of deceased vehicles were scattered.

The morning promised to have some exciting experiences. We were not in any sort of heavy safari country but there were some animals we hoped to see. Monkeys were a strong possibility, said our driver, and we will see hippo's for sure. Hippo's we did see. We stopped at the river where they were known to be – we left the buses, tied up our hair in whatever scarf we had (or extra skirt, as in my case) to keep off the dust and stay cooler, and quietly made our way down to the river. The silence of vast space was again noted, a waterfall tumbled invitingly, adding special overtones of peace. "Be very quiet," warned our driver, "the hippo's will not be alarmed if we move slowly and do not introduce any unusual noises."

There they were, many of them, content, brown against brown water, reddish brown land, a mono-color landscape. Grunts of peaceful contentment passed between them. This was not a hippo in a zoo! This was his land! We were the ones to see him "at home." A satisfying feeling, a moment to just put myself where I belonged, part of the hugeness and yet smallness of this planet, a little speck which makes a difference just as a hippo does with his life in the river, at times supplying food for the lion, always fertilizing the river, which in turn fertilizes the bank. We all felt the chain of life here – a calm, unstoppable cycle.

Around the area grew plant life very different from roadside growth, for here there was some moisture, vines grew stronger, taller, and you knew that in the evening other animals would be coming to the brink for water, their footprints were everywhere. We stayed there watching a long time and were reluctant to leave. The need for water and shade did more to get us back to the bus than desire to leave this place.

We had the "head count" to be sure everyone was back, and took off, we thought! Then there was a crash! Glass breaking and "water" dribbling down over the windows. It seemed the driver had mistaken the height of our luggage atop the bus and a branch had easily swept the precious supplies off the bus roof. Much consternation ensued about whether we would have enough water for the day, but all in all, we decided that with the three buses we could divvy up and would have enough and we should go on.

We were glad for the breeze we created even though it was hot. We passed astonishing termite mounds. There were so many (no wonder there was almost no rotting wood around) and with them also there were fields of cotton. This amazed me that cotton would be grown in such desolate looking fields; a shack here and there to house the pickings while they waited to be picked up and taken to processing and market. It was a "get what you can" operation, no feeling of a proper harvest with remunerative rewards, but more a little here and a little there, just eking out what you could. My mind went to

Chapter 22: Cameroon

the cotton fields in the Carolina's or the tobacco fields in Virginia where the abundance of the crop was evident and you felt there would be a fair return for the labor – here it was getting enough just to survive.

We were headed for a stopping place for lunch – to picnic of course. It turned out that one of the drivers was from the village where we turned in and there was a fine large tree at the entrance where we could park our buses, and even better, a spring (which the drivers partook of, but none of us chose to drink from it). We had to scatter into the bushes for what my family calls the "P" stop. Much easier for the men, but manage we did, and accepted it as the normal thing to do.

The villagers came out cautiously when they saw our buses, their "fences" were simply six by eight foot high woven grass – in plentiful supply – and then stabilized with skinny tree posts. It made a wobbly construction but it did keep out unwanted animals and keep in the wanted ones. The villagers were solemn at first, not coming too close, just staring, and as we smiled and beckoned to them they came closer, keeping their children behind their legs … of course, that was the childrens' choice – nothing different about human nature there!

The little stone slabs around the small fires were typical of kitchen equipment found in all the villages. There was no trash, no ugly litter – there was plenty of that closer to bigger towns where more "sophisticated" products would be available such as coke, packaged chips, etc.

At each village, a bell hung up on a pole, much as farms at home in the early days used to call in the field hands or announce the meals or emergencies. Here, they were usually large enough to be heard by the next village and this is how they communicate warnings or ask for help (perhaps to cope with a brush fire, for instance, or summon a healer). I forgot to ask if they had different bell signals for different needs. It would seem likely they did.

After lunch we mounted again, refreshed, and went on to our goal – the visit to the town of Engoundere, a rather important grass-fenced town where the FON (much like mayor or even king) had requested our visit. He really wanted to connect with American politics and perhaps American benefits, I'm not sure which.

We broke down about two more times, which gave us the opportunity to get to know our fellow passengers intimately for there is an element of camaraderie which develops when you all experience the same dilemma; there is something to be said for

Rainbow's End

being in the same boat heading for the same goal. I understand the bonding afforded by the RAT system at VMI or boot camp in the military better now.

We finally arrived, entering the opening in the grass "wall." We raised a lot of dust but were quickly surrounded by the happy people, with much gesturing and smiling they began to provide us with fine musical entertainment. We joined them, in a little sort of soft shoe dancing in the soft earth.

African instruments create sounds I particularly enjoy (though that is not for everyone). The rhythmic bells on their ankles, the long tubes of the horns produce deep tones. Rhythm is the essence of their music, the tempo often increases as enthusiasm builds or even the heat on the drums brings their tones higher. This was just a preliminary welcome, the real music and dancing would come after lunch. Actually, it was more of the same, just more of it with more people involved!

We were invited to enter the hut provided to house us for lunch. Simple tables were covered with oilcloth (to my surprise) and the food was colorfully offered in huge gourd bowls – absolutely lovely things with the lids woven of colorful straw. There was goat stew in one, rice in another, sweet potatoes in yet the third, and even bright green lettuce (which none of us dared eat) and folding chairs were placed around for our use. Our hosts ate too, at least the entourage chosen to escort us did.

The FON did not join us for the meal. The plan, it seemed, was to finish eating and then go to a bigger hut where more concentrated musical entertainment was arranged in a corral type setting outside and the FON would meet us there. Or we would meet him.

So, after lunch we were invited to follow our hosts. The ambassador went first of course with two aides following him with the chair he had used at lunch. We gathered in a receiving line to meet the FON at last. He was very gracious, imposingly tall and dressed completely in white, covered head to toe, and standing in high heeled white pumps. His shiny black face showed only sparkling happy eyes – white cloth covering his nose and chin (like Arab women). It was comparatively cool inside, and I was amused by the fact that there, standing in a corner (with an electric cord snaking mysteriously out a back door) was an electric fan. We chatted with him for a while. He was delighted to find so many of us spoke French. As we were asked to go to the "terrace" to watch the dancing I noticed he did not join us nor let his people see him. He never left the hut, but left us in charge of his staff who were notably attired in splendid robes and carrying tall spears (a la Cecil B. deMille).

Chapter 22: Cameroon

The ambassador, unfortunately for him, was given a great chair (the same one carried out from inside) and seated out in front of us all which unfortunately placed him directly in the sun – a place of honor in which he politely suffered for three hours! Some of the FON's bearers around us folded onto the ground and fell asleep. It was probably a much bigger lunch than they were used to and I think also some of them had had beer to drink.

We were all getting a bit groggy, but the dancers seemed to be getting a second wind! Our drivers were getting nervous about getting back to our evening location before it got dark. We found out later WHY … but the end did come and we applauded enthusiastically. The wonderful circle of colorful clothing was so festive, and their delight at having us was evident.

The FON reappeared to say goodbye and again disappeared through his own doorway, which led to who knew what. I imagined there may have even been a Mercedes back there for him, along with the electric plug.

Our buses left in the typical whirl of dust and we were off, but not for long. A tire blew. This time we were in a village and not on the roadside and a small semblance of market was still open in the evening hour. One shop caught my eye because it had small bronze figures in the window. On entering I was thrilled to find, in a corner, a bronze horse like the ones I had seen at the Quinta. There was only one large one and I joyously bought it. I knew as soon as I picked it up that it was not going to be an easy thing to get back home, certainly it would not tuck into my suitcase. But have it I would! Several of us bought other souvenirs there and some bought cloth from the market on the street. There was a laundry house where the women were gathered together to scrub on their stones and chat as the children ran around. In about an hour we were finally told the bus had been repaired.

Night was indeed falling and down the road we went only to find, all too soon, that the lights on the bus were not working. That was why the driver had been so agitated. He had known that, but was quite willing to pretend all was well. But Kathleen said absolutely NO! "You stop," she said. "We will all squeeze into two buses with lights and the darkened bus can come behind." If we were not too safe in the daytime, night was even worse – a time to really play with the roads it seemed, among the locals. Enough wrecks on the side of the road proved it. Kathleen was probably saving our lives.

Rainbow's End

We sang songs to keep up our spirits and just when we were about a mile from bed one of the now two buses called it quits. This time, only a half mile from the Quinta, it was decided that we would walk the rest of the way rather than wait for the drivers to make repairs. I had to carry my wonderful, heavy horse (Don Quixote) because the driver said if he had to leave it on the bus the statue would surely disappear.

We only had one more breakdown, but that was the next day just as we were all caravanned into the airport. A tire blew. Again. But this time, all we had to do was thank our drivers and say goodbye.

When I saw the little plane we were to return to Yaounde in I wished that there were some arrangement to place flares in the sky in case of breakdown. Again, the age of the plane was not reassuring, but look … I am here, so I must have made it! When the girls said goodbye to me as I prepared to fly back to America, Katherine, the oldest, handed me a tiny one-inch bronze deer made by the artist who had created my horse, and said, "I want you to have this." I knew how much it meant to her and questioned whether she really wanted to give that up. Today, it is in my home, as treasured as my own purchase that day.

NOTE: This trip was a personal journey for me. Mother had so many memories of her life there when her father was a rancher near the Kimberly diamond mines. She attended a convent nearby from the age of 12 to 18—those very formative years. Her father, a veteran rancher, had had to leave his own ranch in Nebraska when a new law went into effect there to fence your lands and keep your cattle in. It was the last straw to a difficult time—so when his uncle in England offered him a job managing a ranch in Africa he accepted.

It may seem a "fur piece" to us to go to Southern Africa from Nebraska but perhaps to a young Englishman, Africa was not any further from England than Nebraska was.

Six years on the ranch in Africa and a devastating flood washed it away. One of the memories Mother tells is of watching all her books go floating over the fields, including a copy of Lewis Carroll's Alice in Wonderland, given to her by the author who lived nearby! Then the uncle decided not to try to restore the ranch and Mother and her parents and siblings came home to Fredericksburg to live on the family estate and traded ranching for apple orcharding.

Chapter 22: *Cameroon*

The grandparents, too, joined them for great grandfather had just retired from twenty-five years as manager of the Hearst Ranch at San Simeon before the son's castle was built, of course. Mother lived there until she married my father, a foreign service officer, and they lived abroad for twenty-five years, but never in Africa.

Chapter 23
God says Florida?

Fred found himself inexplicably losing his energy and joie de vivre. He was fighting through it, going to exercise classes, seeing a chiropractor regularly, doing his best to get his energy back until, in 1999, he collapsed while playing golf with our neighbor, Dr. Ken Glover. Kin was an ophthalmologist, but recognized that Fred needed immediate emergency treatment and called me and took us to the hospital. Fred's examination revealed he had a leaking valve in his heart and within four days he had a quintuple bypass and a valve replacement.

It was during this time of medical crisis with Fred that I also experienced some medical challenges. After ten years of hard labor at Fall Hill, I had worn out the meniscus in my right knee and, when it became apparent I couldn't walk through the supermarket and balked at going to reach the milk at the other end of the store, I knew I was facing a knee replacement. The first operation required only a partial knee replacement and we all looked forward to a quick recovery since my bones were so strong, but the pain that I experienced continued unremittingly and it was soon discovered that I had a serious multiple resistant staff infection. We proceeded immediately with antibiotics with no good result. The surgeon suggested a second operation to open the knee and replace the partial with a full replacement while treating the infection aggressively, but that didn't work either. I was in the operating room again for the third time in three months to open the original wound and actively flush it with antibiotics. That didn't work either. The fourth attempt at a solution was to submit myself to daily intravenous antibiotic drips administered in a hospital because insurance would not cover it if it was done at home. What was I to do?

For the next four months, I arrived at Mary Washington Hospital in Fredericksburg at 7 a.m. and stayed until 3 p.m. seven days a week. They would not order the antibiotic from the pharmacy until I arrived in the morning. It could not be prepared unless the patient was ready for it. It had to be that fresh. This was, after all, the last stand effort. I could walk with a walker, but my right leg was in pain all the time. I cried often. At first I took a taxi to and from the hospital, then friends did the trip, but then I got stubborn and began to drive myself. Why not, I have a nice Lincoln and I can drive using my left

Rainbow's End

foot, I decided. I practiced in our cul de sac until I was sure I could do the driving safely and then I drove myself, always arranging for a friend or for my daughter, Lisa, to come over and give Fred lunch. A wonderful friendship developed between me and the valet at the hospital, who would take my car and fetch it for me at 3 p.m. The day I did not pick up my car at 3 p.m. was my birthday (March 11). The valet appeared with my keys in his hand. The port in my arm had become infected and needed replacement, birthday or not, and required a small operation. It had been so painful that I cried and when I emerged from the operating room with a new port, my nurses saw my tears and roundly scolded the doctor for making their Bessie cry. And it's her birthday, they said, as if that made it doubly horrible. No, said I, I'm not having birthdays. I'm too miserable to have birthdays. The nurses said, Oh yes you are – and took me back to my special chair which to my delight and amazement was surrounded by balloons and three home-made cakes. I not only had a birthday – I had one that I'll never forget!

Those same, sweet nurses appeared at Fred's funeral many years later in Fredericksburg. I did recover, of course, and one of those nurses on that birthday, as I was lamenting my fate, whispered in my ear, "Bessie, the other people in this room are not going to recover, but you will." The others in the room were there for blood transfusions and terminal conditions. That was a staggering moment.

At first, Fred's recovery looked fairly hopeful but it did not continue, and he slowly declined, dementia beginning to take over as well. I tried to keep everything going but my own energy was flagging and I was discouraged. So, when I prayed, I sincerely told God I could not take care of Fred anymore without better help and God's answer was "Go to Florida." I was very surprised and said, "Why Florida, God? That flat state down there with old people is better than here in my beautiful Virginia?" God chuckled. He repeated, "Go to Florida." So I got up from the sofa and went to the phone to call my travel agent. I asked her "How can I see Florida with an invalid?" She suggested I drive to Jacksonville, book a comfortable ship cabin with a veranda and travel the inland waterways for two weeks. When I told Fred that we were going, he asked me how much it would cost. I told him $4,000 and he shook his head very definitely NO! He was not going to pay $4,000 to sit on a boat and do nothing. I was so frustrated, I stamped my foot and blurted out, "Well, if you won't take a boat ride, will you let me drive you around Florida?" He said he would love it, and in three days we were off. He had nearly always accepted my impetuous ultimatums. I packed the car, including our toffee-colored cocker spaniel,

Chapter 23: God says Florida?

Peter, and went off without having any idea what my route would be. I decided to take 95 and get to Jacksonville and do the research from there.

The second night we arrived in Florida at Amelia Island and we checked into a hotel near the ocean. Fred went to bed and I walked to the beach with the dog. It was an electric moment. The sun was setting. There were surfers tackling the waves and on my right, seemingly coming out of the sand, was a three-masted schooner with its sails up, circling around for an hour into the ocean and then returning down that magical strip of sand to a land I did not know. I stood, transfixed, and said "God, this is indeed a beautiful place. I think you may have something." By the next morning, I had done my research with the help of the concierge at the hotel and planned a route starting on that east side of Florida, crossing over on I-4 to the west, going all the way down to the Everglades, crossing back and going north again to Jacksonville. That trip took us two weeks. I simply stopped when tired – we'd have a lovely dinner – a long evening – and I would find out about the town that we were in.

After the first week, I had seen several retirement villages and began to get the idea that that kind of living would be an answer. So, in Jacksonville, I looked at three of them – Fleet Landing, Carriage House and Vicar's Landing. They seemed almost just right, but not quite, so with brochures under my arm, I drove back to Fredericksburg, put Fred to bed, and called a dear neighbor to tell her I was home. She said, "Bess, did you see Cypress Village? You know a couple who moved there ten years ago. In fact, he was the assistant manager for the City of Fredericksburg, and they love it at Cypress!" She and her husband visited them every year at Cypress Village. She emphasized that Florida is a wonderful state and I should pursue my search and look at Cypress Village. It took me three minutes to pick up the phone and call marketing at Cypress Village and reserve an apartment for us to look it over. The day we arrived, I was taken on a tour. Fred went halfway with me and then wanted lunch, so I told him to order for me and I would meet him in the dining room. I finished the tour of apartments and houses and joined Fred, telling him that I thought the apartment overlooking the big lake, which happened to be just one floor up from the couple from Fredericksburg would be perfect. He said, "No, I want that third little house we saw." I was very surprised, thinking Fred was not even aware of what was going on. So I told him to order dessert and I would be back. Quickly, I returned to the agent and asked her which one was the third house. We hopped in her car and she took me to see it again. All she had to do was open the front door and

Rainbow's End

I could look through the house to the back to the lake and to the fountain. I figured I could fix anything else, and we bought it. While signing the papers for the mortgage, I said to Fred, "You know your son said not to buy anything big without calling him." Fred answered, "I don't do everything my son tells me," so we finished the transaction. Fred's son, Gregg, who is a licensed financial advisor and a wonderful friend, had been managing our portfolio since Fred's retirement. He had given us good advice all along the way, but in this instance, Fred seemed to know this was the right thing.

We stayed at Cypress for three days before going back to Fredericksburg to prepare for Lisa's wedding at 210 Brooke Drive and then our big move to Florida. The second day at Cypress, we were invited to the bi-weekly cocktail party and our agent introduced us to several of our future neighbors, including Joe Bracewell and Chuck Walker. They invited us to church the next evening for the church social supper. It was the First Christian Church of the Beaches in Jacksonville Beach, and to our delight, was the same denomination of the church where Fred had been an elder for fifteen years and where we were married. That Wednesday evening, I was invited to practice with the choir while Fred went to men's Bible class and I joined the choir that night. I knew that was going to be our church. It was warm and fuzzy, and we even had a meal with the new minister who had just been hired and was being housed at Cypress Village until he found a home to buy. There was no question from that first meeting on, that the church was going to be ours. We loved everything about it. It was God's message to me that I had made the right decision. Oh, and by the way, Cypress Village has the incredible advantage of being one mile from Mayo Hospital and Clinic.

Having made the decision to buy at Cypress Village, it was my intention to simply move here for a year at the most and Fred would get better and we would return to Virginia. That was the plan. So, I made arrangements with Cypress Village for refurbishment of our new home here while we returned to Virginia for Lisa's May 2003 wedding at Brooke Drive. After the beautiful wedding in a tent on the lawn, Fred and I began to plan our move. The first thing I did was ask Lisa and her new husband, Mike Parrish, to move into Brooke Drive while we were in Florida. They loved the idea and so the plans were underway for our move. I wasted no time, ordered appropriate furniture, and by June, we were moving in.

By this time, due to his advanced dementia and physical deterioration, Fred needed someone with him all the time. I found a wonderful Filipino caretaker, Lynn Duve.

Chapter 23: God says Florida?

She filled the bill to perfection and stayed with us for six years until Fred's death in 2008. During that time, of course, I realized we would not be moving back to Virginia. Lisa and Mike went back to Lisa's home in Fredericksburg and I was able to sell the home at Brooke Drive for an enormous profit. Lisa and Mike have since built themselves a beautiful colonial home outside Fredericksburg, where I have a separate apartment waiting for me whenever I wish to use it.

The day we moved in to our new home at Cypress Village, I found that the work I'd asked for had been done exactly as I wished. Things all fit pretty much as I had imagined they would. I brought very little from my house, as I expected to go back there, and had ordered furniture specifically for Florida. The celery colored walls were just right and the wood floors were a big improvement from the rug that had been there before. I was pleased and so was Fred. We made up his bed as quickly as possible and he said, "I think this will be a good place."

A year later, I had my piano brought here, knowing by then that I was going to stay. When the piano arrived, Fred looked at it and said, "Okay, that means we're staying."

My neighbors came over to greet me when we moved in. One of those was Joe Bracewell, who told me that his wife was bedridden and ill. I offered to sit with her if he ever needed someone, as I was a trained hospice worker. He was very helpful unloading the furniture and we walked our dogs together in the morning, soon becoming good friends.

During those first years, Fred would have sharp dips in his blood pressure and pass out, becoming dehydrated no matter how much he seemed to drink. The Duval County rescue squad arrived within six minutes whenever we called, recognizing the immediacy of our need to get Fred to the hospital. They were and are a remarkable medical support. I had a few medical issues of my own as the years went on.

I needed another knee replacement, this time of my left knee, and finally opted for the surgery in spite of my horrific fears to do so, not wanting to repeat the same experience with MRSA. This time, however, it was a piece of cake, and within six weeks, I was dancing again. The other medical concern was the need for a hysterectomy, which also was smoothly accomplished. Post-care and therapy here are excellent.

Joe's wife, Betty, died within that first year and he and I found our evenings very lonely. I had told Joe that I did not cook. I did not tell him I was a trained French chef because I really had decided that I was going to give myself a few hours of non-domestic

Rainbow's End

time every day and see what I did with the time. So I had, indeed, arrived in Florida with two pots and pans and a minimal number of dishes. Fred loved fast food and so fast food was going to be our diet, but Fred was also asleep by 5 o'clock p.m., in fact, pretty much slept twenty hours a day.

One evening Joe asked me over for dinner and I was watching him cook. He was mixing something in such a way that I couldn't help but say, "Wouldn't it be better if you did it this way?" He looked up and said, "I thought you said you did not cook." I told him I did say that, but I did not say I could not cook, and then the truth was out. We shared many more dinners, some at his house and some at mine. I often took meals over to Joe's after Fred had gone to sleep, as Lynn Duve was willing to stay a few hours longer in the evening.

Joe took me to church every Wednesday and Sunday and that was and is a huge part of my life now. Fred only went a few times in the very beginning, but was unable to walk well enough to go. I'm in the choir and active in several other church activities, even taking on the leadership in my home of a small group called Basic Family which is for the purpose of getting to know each other on a more personal level. Joe is a part of this Basic Family group as well, and in fact, has over the years become family to me.

During the years of Fred's continuing decline and following the death of Joe's wife, the two of us became a great comfort to one another, and we still remain close. We both love to travel and take many short trips. We love to dance and cook and we attend all the church meetings and retreats, as well as the social events at Cypress Village. As the years go by, Joe's hearing has decreased markedly and my sight has decreased as well – we've learned to compromise and accept changes as they happen.

Often, when I look into Joe's eyes, I can see my Jim looking back at me. I feel cared for and loved by this man who is so different from Jim and yet has much of the same heart. During the first few months after Fred and I arrived, Fred could still carry on a short conversations. He and Joe found that

Chapter 23: God says Florida?

their careers had been almost identical in the military. They had both entered without a finished education, gotten their degrees through the military, and both were sponsored to attend Officers Candidate School. Each of them retired as Majors. They also had each been assigned particularly important missions during their careers, Joe's with the Berlin Airlift and the his mapping expeditions around the world including Vietnam, and Fred's duties as a translator in the Intelligence Service, sent to help bring the Hungarians out from behind the Iron Curtain. So, these two men were highly appreciated by the military and served extraordinary careers. They were both champions for America and felt that any sacrifice was worth fighting a threat to freedom. Joe still feels very much that way.

Fred's funeral at Arlington was a dramatic experience for me of how blessed our country is to have heroes who will protect it. The beautiful service to go to his graveside for the burial was led by six horses and the hearse was accompanied by a military honor guard unit with the family walking behind. In fact, it was particularly memorable artistically because of the placement of Fred's grave at the bottom of the hill. It had been reserved in 1976 when Fred buried his wife, Lila, there, and his daughter, Dana's ashes were also spread there. As we walked down to his gravesite from the top of the hill overlooking Washington D.C., down the steep incline curving into the field where Fred's grave was prepared, it was a perfect day, and as we rounded the curve approaching the gravesite, the taps were blowing from the woods and you could only hear the spreading sound. There was no visible source for it. It was simply everywhere. It could not have been more moving. None of us had ever experienced a military funeral. We were not prepared for the deep honor Fred was receiving. After taps was played, there was a 21 gun salute. I had requested that his son, Gregg, be presented with the flag.

So, in my experience, I've had a gentle, sensitive giant named Jim who gave me the three most important treasures of my life, and a hero named Fred, who came at a critical time when I needed him so badly to help me with my family, and now Joe, a good man, in the quiet of old age. Joe and I walk our separate paths, but we walk them together.

Speaking of walking, early in our friendship, Joe and our friends, Chuck and Faye Walker, sponsored me to go to the Walk to Emmaus! This was a pivotal event in my life and I felt God's love and direction right in my heart with no barriers between us. It was at Emmaus that I learned that I had to not only forgive my brother, Butler, for some very unpleasant legal quarrels we had over mother's estate, but that I had to forgive myself for anything I may have done to fan the flame. Through Emmaus and prayer, I have found peace within myself and direction in my life. Joe's son, Reese, gave me a lovely painting of the Emmaus story after the walk. I was touched by his thoughtfulness.

Another thing Reese did that touched me was the day we went to Bette's grave on the first anniversary of her death. The ceremony at this large cemetery was to commemorate those who had passed away during the previous year by placing a paper angel on a Christmas tree and having the name announced and prayed for. Reesie had come to me with the angel in his hand for me to put my mother's name on it, recognizing that she, too, had died that year. It meant a great deal to me as I had not been able to be in Virginia when she died.

Chapter 24
Cypress Village & My Church Family

Here at Cypress Village, I've had the most wonderful parties on my patio. A New Year's party with dancing and glittering lights was a special success. I cooked the Southern black-eyed peas and greens, which I'd never done before, but I'd learned it was a Southern tradition, so I'd better do it. The black-eyed peas were so appreciated that all the food I had ordered from Publix, such as prepared sandwiches, was not even touched. So few of us now, at Cypress Village, have the energy to give a party that I followed this one up with a Halloween party and invited my sister from Texas. It was at this party that I learned she is very shy, and in retrospect, I remembered that every time my mother entertained and insisted on her daughters attending, my sister would push me into the parlor first. Jenny's costume was a red sheet covering her from head to toe, little red slippers, a devil's tail sewn to the rear-end and two little horns on her head. She had only cut holes for her eyes. There was no way to recognize her and the forty friends who were there still wonder what she looked like. She never unveiled. When it came time to eat, Joe's son got a pair of scissors and cut a hole for Jenny's mouth, and fed her a hamburger bit by bit through that hole. Jenny was enchanted. We had marvelous dancing with a DJ whose triplet children helped me with serving and clearing the table. I think they were about eleven years old at that time – two girls and a boy. Of course, we had a costume contest. One of my guests arrived so wonderfully disguised that I finally had to ask her who she was. She was my dog's sitter and she came hunched over with a crooked cane, a ghastly old hag mask with warts, and a huge hat. Even Chuck Walker was incognito for several hours before we discovered who he was. I had a cauldron of dry ice smoking on the patio. We had witches and ghouls and I believe the party is still talked about today.

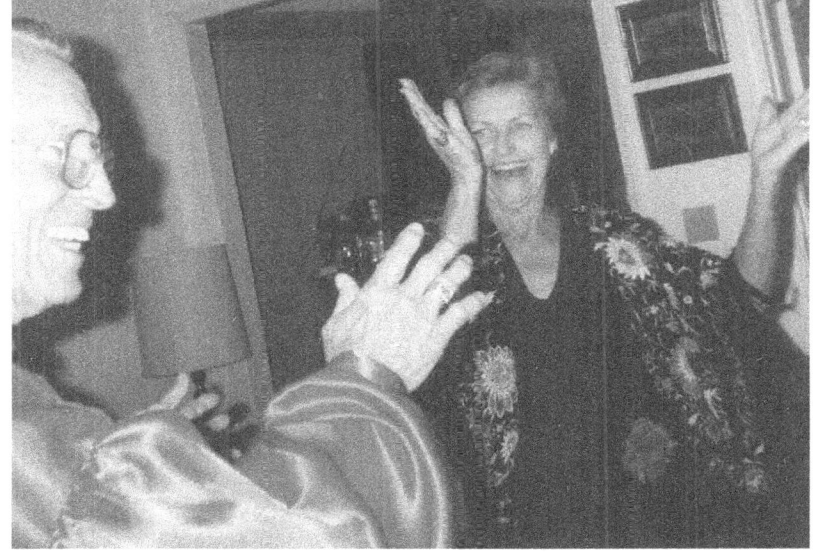

Rainbow's End

On a fourth of July, Joe and I entered our pets into the dog show and won first prize for the costumes we'd decked them out in. Joe and I had put together a wonderful patriotic red, white and blue for Bella, his white Bichon, jacket and hat included, and for my cocker spaniel, Peter, a flamboyant red white and blue statement – and the two of them together enhanced one another.

Two years after Fred died, my cocker spaniel, Peter passed away. The house was so lonely. I missed Peter, but couldn't make myself get another dog. My son told me, when you're ready for a dog, please look up a Havanese – mixture of Bechon, Chi Tzu and Poodle – they are quiet, laid back and devoted to their owners. I was walking through the house and feeling the emptiness one day and I looked up Breeders of Havanese on the computer. Up came two sources, one in Atlanta and one in Tampa. I pulled up the one in Atlanta and the strip of puppies that came up on my screen had five little babies – black and white. The very first one, named Asia, looked at me and said, "You're mine." The phone rang and the breeder was calling me. Somehow, she knew I was on her website, and she asked, "Are you looking at our puppies?" Asia, she told me, would be old enough to leave in eight days. "She can be on the plane to Jacksonville by Monday, May 10, with all her shots and everything you need. May 10 was Fred's birthday. I said, "Oh, that would be wonderful! How much is she?" I gasped when she replied $2,000. Okay, I thought, what have I done? But she was mine already. I would just not travel for three months.

May 10th rolled around and Joe was sitting with me having coffee. I said, "Joe, could you take me to the airport?" Oh, he asked, who are we meeting? "It's not a person – it's a puppy." A puppy! Why are you getting a puppy! He got up and walked out with his dog, Bella. He said, "This will ruin our relationship." Ten minutes later he came back and said, "I'm sorry. I've been thinking and you have every right to enjoy a dog as much as I enjoy Bella."

Molly is so glad to see me when I come home. She cuddles me anytime I want. I never want to be without her. She's turned into my little sidekick. Joe even likes her now. Bella is her mother and lets her do all sorts of things. Bella taught Molly to bark. They love to roughhouse.

The next year with Molly was the October dog parade and I dressed up as a witch with a tall black hat and black cape, plopped Molly into that caldron that I'd used at the party some years before, picked up a big wooden spoon, and called Molly the Witch's brew. That was a hit.

Chapter 24: Cypress Village & My Church Family

We look forward to those parades every year. There are regular dances at Cypress and on the first Saturday of the month – they even have three professional young dance teachers to dance with the ladies who do not have partners. We also have a strong connection to the University of North Florida music program, mainly because one of our residents, Coralie Williams, directs or manages these events and gets promising young musicians to perform at them. I have heard some breathtaking talent at these events – singers I know I will hear about for the rest of my life.

We have travel-log lectures, sing-alongs, various types of book clubs. The one I particularly enjoy is the Blind Book Club. That may sound like an oxymoron, but we share our books on tape put out by the Library for the Blind and most of us depend on that reading for all our books. It is a huge blessing. We can even ask for certain books to be taped for us and the Director of Books for the Blind at the Jacksonville Library, Chris Eaton, goes out of his way to accommodate us. This year the government cut back on their supplies and Chris can't record a book until he gets a free tape, so he has to juggle to get what we want for books.

At least once a month, we have a special meal celebrating something at Cypress, like the Oktoberfest, or China Day ... you never know what it's going to be ... I love their off-the-wall themes, and then the residents who can, come with their memories of those themes or they might have a display of their possessions that fit the theme. It's a nice way to celebrate.

Of course, Cypress offers regular exercise classes and swimming exercise and walks on the beach once in a while with our director and free trips to go shopping for groceries twice a week. As you can see, my dear reader, it is an active, satisfying place to live.

Cypress village has offered me many opportunities to lead singing or to sing solos or to talk up life here with new, perspective residents. Joe and I love walking around our numerous picturesque lakes with our dogs, each lake with a different tone to it. One lake is "owned" by the huge white egret who lives on the roof of our dock. He lords it over all the life beneath him and I even, yearly, go and scrape up his guano to use to fertilize my garden. My own private lake, I call it, in the back of my house has only about nine houses on it and we face a protected tract of land that goes on through to Mayo property. Deer often appear in the evening on the edge of the lake, coming for water. We have five resident wild turkeys, fox, raccoons, an occasional eagle and osprey and unwelcome alligators. The alligators are a threat to our dogs but after all, this is Florida – their natural habitat. Once they are four feet long, we're allowed to ask for their removal by the association, and they are taken to another location. Alligators are the reason, though, that our beautiful geese with their numerous babies seldom make it to adulthood.

One of my tremendous delights of living here is standing at the edge of the ocean on Jacksonville Beach, which is only ten minutes away and one of the finest beaches in the world. It is fine, hard sand and was even the locale for car races years before Daytona became the center for that sport. Now that I don't drive, I still get to spend several hours a week on my ocean because I have a ride to church on Wednesdays for supper and choir and, instead of eating supper, I go to the beach and watch the sunset behind the First Christian Church of the Beaches. The other time is on Sundays – again, I can extend my ride to the church by going down to the shore after Bible Class during the social hours. One of the parishioners, when he sees me, always asks me what did the ocean tell you today? I answer that some days it's playing like a quiet symphony with a Grieg theme and other days it's an absolute Wagner!

I was empowered recently to explore my discovery of the deep roar that the ocean has as a constant background to the surf sound by a sudden realization while listening to the composer Grieg on NPR, that he, too, had heard it and knew it well. That roar permeates the first movement of one of his pieces. It truly excites me that I'm not alone in hearing that roar. I wrote a poem that describes my feelings about the ocean's roar and a "whole lot more."

Chapter 24: Cypress Village & My Church Family

Listening to the Ocean

I'm listening to the ocean and hearing a new roar
A low persistent humming
That I've never heard before

This is not the lighter rhythm of waves upon the shore
Topped by windblown plumes of stallions
Leaping from the ocean's core

This is a deep, unending score with drums and cellos followed yet by more
In depths of the ocean, new mountains are formed
Volcanoes are erupting, new islands in a storm

Perhaps it's earth's creation, roaring on and on
Perhaps it's earth's creation, roaring on and on

My life is much like the foregoing poem. I'm hearing things I've never heard before. I'm reflecting, also, on the tribute to my mother, calling her a Lighthouse on the Shore. How appropriate that we have another similarity that I could only discover at this stage of my life. As my eyesight has dimmed, new light has opened my senses. I am enjoying a time of discovery and heightened introspection, using tools that were lying dormant before. Different vibes in the air identify new friends, old friends, even family – how they walk, the tone of their voices, the energy of their spirit – I can even detect sadness, anger and joy before ever a word is spoken. The myriad perfumes of the garden are magnified, the scents of each flower overwhelmingly beautiful. Seen through my new vision, each pansy in my garden becomes an angel. The awareness of sound even guides my feet over rough ground. I can feel the earth through my body, through my hands, through my listening. I have less sight physically, but my spiritual and emotional sight has grown to such a satisfying level that the living of each day is richer than ever before.

Chapter 25
Bessie's Poetry

Lament for Prayer
(September 2012)

*Jesus is weeping
As He kneels down above
Watching all His children
With His heart so filled with love*

*Why are my children whispering?
What are they afraid to say?
I don't hear them praying
Before they go out to play?*

*Why don't they gather together
And cheer now for their Lord?
To protect them and to guide them,
Like they did before?*

*Why can't they share their faith now
That had come with them to school?
I want to be there when they're tempted
And show them what to do.*

*Dear Father, help me.
Where did I go wrong?
Why is there so much fear today?
We used to be so strong.*

Chapter 25: Bessie's Poetry

New World
(October 2012)

I cannot see the world today
The way I saw it yesterday
A burst of sunshine glistens
On the last remaining view
Casting prisms in variety
Ever-changing, always new!

So many times
(September 2012)

So many times
In life's design
We simply wonder
   why
   why
   why

There is no answer
No -- not for us
The challenge is
To live in trust

We do not know
But nor did He
Yet down He went
On bended knee
And let His Father
Weep for Him
Freeing us all
From mortal sin

Birth

(My birth in Saltillo, Mexico)

One babe ... one cry
Now entered in this world
Amidst the screaming sounds of battle

One babe now born
Did bring her mother's heart
Some peace ... some safe relief

The streets outside the quiet room
Belied the birth of love
Cried only doom

What forces led deep angered men
To lift a gun
To shoot a friend?

While grief lay smoldering in the streets
Not doused by violence
Nor spent by man's repents

A vanity prevailed
As the babe did sleep
Her Mother's arms so safe

Deep within the fiber of this newest life
A million seeds were finding space
To shape a future growth

The cry became a voice
For feelings planted deep
To burst their bounds from shackled fear
Warlike anger and man's deceit

*Continued to invade the child's peace
Which found no place for quick release*

*Until at last she dared to speak
And from those wounds of war
Rose "she" … a child no more*

Grief

*A cradle rocks
The babe's not there
A Mother all alone
Upstairs*

*A Father sorrows
Tears unshed
His grief too deep,
Too deep, unsaid.*

My Prayer
(2007)

*How do I know when God is speaking?
How do I know what He has to say?*

*When the joy of peace can fill my being,
And I hear the sound of silence when I pray.*

*When His cherished love spreads warmly around me,
And consuming turmoil melts away.*

*That's when I know that God is speaking.
That's when I know we've talked today.*

The Cherry
(2007)

The sweetness of a cherry passes my lips
What topsy turvy sweetness is this?
To savor a cherry in a winter clime?
How sublime.

When...
When I see a winter tree against the setting sun,
I know what truth can be
And strength comes from simplicity.

When I lift my eyes to see blue skies,
And watch the stretching vapor trails
I know the power of man's desires.
When I hear a child's trusting laugh,
I feel laughter in my own heart
And know the lightness of joy.

When I sense the rage of a coming storm,
I know my life is part of every living thing
And safety comes from faith within.

When I watch a breaking wave upon the shore,
I know that life must change
And only change brings life.

When I taste sweet rain upon my lips
I know that growth is sure
And the sweetness of living is a gift.

When I hear clear birdsong fill the air,
I know the need for sharing
And the bonds of caring.

Friendship
(1980)

From friendship grows another self
Much surer, stronger, wiser
Than just my own aloneness does allow.
From friendship grows a love to share

My own thick walls stripped down
A place to trust, to stand quite bare, a place to trust.

Don't Ask

Don't ask to know the future
Don't ask to know what for

Each moment is your destiny
Embrace it, live it well
And take a step towards God's throne
Where one day you will dwell

Life's challenges are precious gifts
Though storms may seem unfair
Small, even whispered, blessings,
Surround you everywhere.

Feel It

Mist from river's cauldron
Snowfall's feather lightness
Vapor trails stretching
A sky swept clear and blue

Hail's insistent tapping
Ice skates sharply etching

Freight trains endless clacking
A curtained, cozy room
A child's cry unheeded
Headlights stringing garlands
On highway's ribboned blackness
Night envelopes soon

A Small Boy's Sandcastle

He's dug a castle deep and wide
With turrets mounting on every side
His little hands have tried and tried
To dig two channels for easy flow
The ocean dug one more below

Small friends have stopped to gaze in awe
While he chisels and shapes to clear every flaw
Then rises in wonder, the crevices filled
His kingdom is perfect
One wave and its stilled

He stands without moving his toes in the sand
The foam of destruction swirls round his fat hand
He's watching the space where his dream world did soar
Then picks up the shovel
Starts digging once more

The Wild Goose

We watched his soar and the descend to make a place among his friends
The sunset glowed a closing hymn to summer's set of happenings
He soared again, seemed not content

Chapter 25: Bessie's Poetry

Unease prevailed his snow white breast
His mate did follow with wings spread wide
Her only wish to follow his glide

He waited, watched
We heard a shot
His fall to ground did rend our hearts
His mate returned to mourn and cry
He lay so still she knew not why

As morning air grew warm and damp
She left his side with loud lament
Her need was strong for distant shores
While others far above did call

My children, grown, may pass this way
As with them I did pass today
They, too, can see the search goes on
When life presents its churning storms

They'll think of me so long ago
When they were small and held my hand
Along the store of drifting sand
Along the path of life's demands

They, too, will hear deep-throated calls
And hold the hands of others small
Who also know that something more
Replenishes our earthly store

They may just stand as I do today
And wonder how life goes astray
Yet seems the same as yesterday

A Child

So much promise lies within the spirit of a child
So much tender feeling is revealed in his care
The growth that he now shows us is a symbol of our own

The needs for which he calls us are not just his alone

He pulls our hand to guide us and to say 'This moment's rare.'
We think we are the teachers, but we're in the child's care.

Fossils White

(An Archeological dig)

Fossils white embedded deep
In cliffs and crevices
All the jagged prehistoric
Refuse and debris of earth's developing

Canyons bare the secrets stored
Life giving rivers cutting to the floor
Undulating stratas
Formed mountains in the silence of a roar

Caves remain which sheltered safe
Encrusted walls with artists skills
Revered as Altamira
Lascaux Shrine to ancient fills

Treasures of our destiny
Saved stories of our lives
We still do search for purpose
As we scrape and chip the lime

Chapter 25: Bessie's Poetry

Redwinged Blackbird

A redwinged blackbird
Bows the stem
Of graceful pampas grass
Such order seems to flow
Around his world
With graceful landings
And artful flights
In orchestrated rhythm
His tension shows
As sun drops low
His flight brings truth to me
Life goes
Hand in hand
With Strife
And cannot be
All free-winged
Flowing ecstasy

Beside a River

Sit beside a river and watch the waters flow
There you'll find a teacher who'll show you how to row

How pass the bending trees and how to safely glide
From one great fallen oak to an eddy on the other side

How to have great patience when the waters rise and rile
To wait and watch – to watch and wait – you'll cross in just awhile

The river knows its purpose. It knows where it has to go.
It can give you all the answers … but finding truth is slow.

Precious Life – Cape Canaveral

We cheer while space craft soar
Gathering of minds reach out
Creating wild machines to explore
Lifting now on cauldrons of power
To circle earth, to seek and probe
The wonders of this universe still untold
Light years of space stretch on and on
Though time and talent spent
The wonder of a single seed
Has not its match yet met

Awakening

Wake to a promise
Of unseen forces
Threatening rain

Blowing hair
Hawks circling high
On a vortex of air

Yesterday's blossom
Old branches fallen

A tumble down shed
An unmade bed

Half-eaten rolls
Worn out clothes

Muddied old shoes
Towels bestrewn

All leave a story
For our minds to bemuse

A Winter's Walk

I walk beside a river under open skies
Mark my steps with patience on the frosted ferns
Listen to the silence of the passing mist
Pause to hear the stretching of the icy limbs

Wonder at the patterns on the frozen floor
Feel the finite smallness of this time and place
Knowing changes bring the force for life
Knowing after darkness comes the glare of light

A Circle

A circle is one never-ending quest
For deeper meaning, deeper love
In God's great universe.
Each truth revealed within ourselves
Gives rise to many more
As circles in a stream they spread
To touch the farthest shore
A circle is one never-ending quest
For deeper meaning, deeper love
In God's great universe.

How Often

How often has a flower bloomed the thoughts you wish to say
How often has a marigold brushed gloom from out your way
A rosebud filled with promise of a future yet unknown
Can lift the sorrow from your heart, and as you look, you're not alone
How often have you watched great waves sweep footprints from the shore

And tumble noble castles made whose fragile walls your dreams did store
Those castles are your memories, which waves cannot destroy
And footprints once upon the shore, remain within- those marks are yours

How often have your child's tears brought longing to your heart
To banish all those ugly fears and fill the space with love
For only loving arms can give your child the strength to know
He has to live with honest thoughts and when he hurts, that's when he grows

The Walnut and my Flower Garden
(Dedicated to my brother, Lynn, who wrote the first line)

"The walnut is a caution flower"
It's sweetness wrapped for none to see
Trying to tell us secretly
That patience builds the strength of trees

The color of chrysanthemums
Can tease as summer ends its stay
Then steadily enhances, no surprises
Spreading long its rich display
The tiger lily's orange flash

Lasts for only for a day
It's fleeting presence a rare delight
Unlike the walnut, a glorious display

www.ingramcontent.com/pod-product-compliance
Lightning Source LLC
Chambersburg PA
CBHW080402170426
43193CB00016B/2787